# Welcome to
# The
# iPad Book

**A**pple's recent launch of the new iPads have made it clear why most people are opting for one these days - both for professional usage at work and as a primary device at home. Its impressive battery life, multi-tasking abilities and incredible high-resolution screen have revolutionised the way we carry out our everyday tasks. **The iPad Book** examines how you can use your iPad to improve every aspect of your life, from the office and home, to being on the move. Apart from apps that will extend the functionality of your device, the book features useful secrets that will help you unleash its full hidden potential. Enjoy exploring what we have enjoyed producing!

# The iPad Book

Imagine Publishing Ltd
Richmond House
33 Richmond Hill
Bournemouth
Dorset BH2 6EZ
☎ +44 (0) 1202 586200
**Website:** www.imagine-publishing.co.uk
**Twitter:** @Books_Imagine
**Facebook:** www.facebook.com/ImagineBookazines

**Head of Publishing**
Aaron Asadi

**Head of Design**
Ross Andrews

**Production Editor**
Sherwin Coelho

**Senior Art Editor**
Danielle Dixon

**Design**
Rachel Shemilt

**Printed by**
William Gibbons, 26 Planetary Road, Willenhall, West Midlands, WV13 3XT

**Distributed in the UK & Eire by**
Imagine Publishing Ltd, www.imagineshop.co.uk. Tel 01202 586200

**Distributed in Australia by**
Gordon & Gotch, Equinox Centre, 18 Rodborough Road, Frenchs Forest,
NSW 2086. Tel + 61 2 9972 8800

**Distributed in the Rest of the World by**
Marketforce, Blue Fin Building, 110 Southwark Street, London, SE1 0SU

Part of the

# iCreate™
bookazine series

# The iPad Book
# Contents

 **Music**

 **Videos**

**Page 10:**
**Your life & iPad**
Discover how your tablet can help make every aspect of your life so much easier

 **Safari**

**50**

 **Settings**

 **App Store**

 **iTunes**

**44**

**85**

**90**

120

**Page 128:**
iBookstore
Make the most of this free
app to ensure efficient
reading on your iPad

# Siri

# Camera

# Photos

# Photo Booth

# Game Center

**Page 168:**
**Essential accessories**
Find out how you can enhance your device and make it an even more flexible tablet

# Newsstand

# iBooks

# Pages

# Keynote

"It's possible to film clips from within iMovie and instantly insert them into your timeline"

# iMovie

# Numbers

# GarageBand

# iPhoto

# Your life & iPad

Apple's stunning new range of iPads can benefit your life in so many ways, regardless of what you are doing or where you are going

**The new iPads offer all of the practical benefits you would want from a tablet.** By releasing three new iPads in the space of six months, Apple really has pushed the envelope of design, innovation and usability in its already vast and reputable range of tablets that are taking the world by storm. Their battery is quoted as offering up to ten hours of power while watching video and listening to music over Wi-Fi, and an impressive nine hours over 3G. The new iPad battery has been proved to out-perform even these ambitious times, and so, for the majority of users, a charger will only be an occasional requirement. The new screens are breathtaking, and once you start surfing complex websites and reading eBooks, other tablets won't feel the same. You may think that a higher resolution screen is no big deal, but when you consider that the screen on a tablet is everything you look at and interact

with, you start to realise that the better it is, the richer your overall experience is going to be. The new iPad also brings with it an improved processor which has been designed to work faster, especially for today's consumer who uses it as a multi-functional device for professional work, productivity and entertainment. For complex games with stunning graphics, it helps to push the entertainment experience along on the millions of pixels that are present. Ultimately, iPads are a popular choice of millions because of the way the hardware and software work seamlessly together and the quality of the materials used. When you pick up an iPad and swipe your finger across the screen, feel the metal cover and immerse yourself in an experience that does not, for one moment, feel like a computer. It quickly becomes clear that this is a rich, immersive and addictive product that's worth its every penny.

# Work

The new iPads have the potential to replace your work laptop for the vast majority of your business tasks

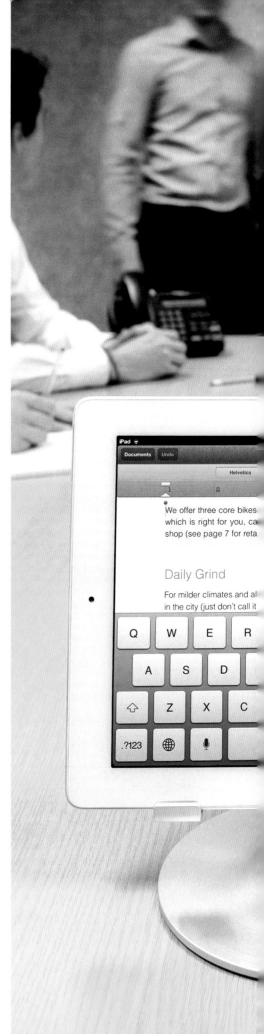

The iPad is not just a tool for surfing the web and entertainment, as it comes with a selection of apps that can help you to be extremely productive. On top of this, there are countless other solutions that will help business people deal with specialist tasks, and even communicate with others in a manner that would have felt like science fiction a couple of years ago. With iOS 6, the calendar can be synchronised with a variety of services, including Google, Exchange and iCloud, and the way it works makes dealing with the busiest of times child's play. You can change appointments by moving them with your finger, and create new meetings with a couple of taps. The presentation is pure Apple, and ensures that your calendar is organised and accurate at all times. The fact that it will be synchronised with your smartphone and desktop also removes much of the administration that is normally required. The Reminders app looks, at first glance, too sparse for those with numerous tasks to complete, but again the stripping away of unnecessary clutter brings your information and tasks to the forefront. The Contacts app is also simple in its design, but capable of letting you build a comprehensive database, and the Notes app follows similar ethos by providing visual simplicity with the ability to create and view massive amounts of content.

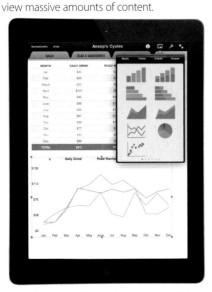

*The combined benefits of the apps that are included with the iPad are plentiful*

As good as the included apps are, there are more sophisticated solutions available from the App Store, some of which rival commercial desktop solutions in the features they offer. Apple's iWork suite of apps are perfect examples of how you can utilise the iPad for work-related tasks. Numbers is a fully functional spreadsheet solution that offers most of the functions that business people require. It has been designed to work perfectly with a touchscreen, and instils in the user a whole new way of working as they become familiar with re-sizing cells and building complex calculations. The files can be exported in Excel format to aid compatibility with the majority of Office systems, and despite the initial learning curve, it is a great example of how an iPad can be used for work. Pages is a word processor that, again, has been designed to work by touch alone. There are many templates built in, but ultimately it will prove useful as a tool to let you create documents when on the move, and it also has the ability to export files in more standard formats. The main advantage, however, is how quick it is to use, and how simple it makes the creation of complex documents that encompass images and lots of formatting. When compared to Word on a desktop, Pages feels more natural and intuitive, and could become your main document creation tool. We should also not forget the effectiveness of the iPad keyboard, which is incredibly efficient thanks to its larger-than-average size and clever word-correction facility.

Keynote is the final tool in the iWork suite. It will let you create presentations without the frustration of dealing with multiple features or a complex interface. It offers the perfect mix of complex production alongside ease of use that makes the experience feel almost too easy. Building presentations will, all of a sudden, feel like a walk in the park and you will be able to create visually pleasing content in half the time. When you consider the cost of each of these apps and the benefits they offer, the iPad soon looks like a serious business tool that you will actually want to use. Add to this the hundreds of even more specialist business apps and solutions that offer desktop-capable performance, and you start to realise that the iPad could replace a laptop for many daily business tasks.

> "The iPad has a selection of apps that can help make your life extremely productive"

# 5 Ways to improve your work life

## 1 Forget the laptop
The iPad can be used for presenting, as well as many other tasks, such as meeting minutes in place of more traditional solutions, so check out what accessories and apps there are, and dispense with your laptop once and for all.

## 2 Invest in apps
Invest in the iWork apps, and you will be more than happy that you did. Numbers, Pages and Keynote offer exceptional value for money, and will come in handy time and time again. They could even replace your current Office document solutions.

## 3 No limits
There are no limits to what you can do with an iPad. If you have a specialist task that needs to be completed, or work in an unusual industry, chances are that there are apps available that are perfectly suited to your requirements.

## 4 Write, don't type
There are situations such as meetings where writing notes is still preferable to typing away on a tablet screen. Invest in a stylus and a note-taking app, and you will soon realise the benefits. It also looks more natural to other attendees, who are less likely to be distracted.

## 5 Be secure
Security will always be paramount when using work-related data on a mobile device. Check with your employer as to what you are allowed to download and carry, and ensure that you have password-protected your iPad.

# Home

**A new iPad could be the perfect household device to keep everyone organised and entertained all of the time**

The coffee table in your lounge probably has a couple of magazines, some flowers and various other objects on it most of the time. However, imagine if it could be a TV, game console or creativity tool, among other things, and still not dominate the room. Well, it can be, and all you need are one of the new iPads. In the house, an iPad is an incredibly flexible and worthy tool which will do almost anything you want it to. For many people it has moved their computing time away from the desktop computer to any room in the house that they are comfortable in.

Apple offers two apps that can help anyone get creative on their iPad when the mood strikes, and the first of note is iPhoto. It is unusually complex for an Apple product, and is not the easiest to get used to, but once you are familiar with it, you will be surprised at just how powerful it is. If you take photos on your

> **"An iPad can serve various functions such as organisation, entertainment, education and networking, making it the ideal device for your home"**

iPhone, they will automatically be uploaded to the Photo Stream service. You can then spend some time tweaking each one and adding myriad effects on your iPad until they are exactly how you want them to be. Once you have the effects in place, you can use the AirPrint technology to print each photo on your printer without ever having to fiddle about with cables. Moreover, you can, of course, share the photos via email or through social networks – all on the iPad. iMovie will need more of your time, but it is a complete

solution that lets you create professional-looking home movies with effects and gimmicks that will make the viewer believe that they are watching something created on a powerful desktop PC. Wherever you want to be in your house, you can create at any time.

Gaming is another entertainment form that is moving away from static locations, and some of the titles available for the iPad are already close to console quality. With Game Centre built in, you can challenge friends and family no matter where they are, and enjoy longer multiplayer escapades with anyone in the world. The games – and indeed, movies and TV programmes – can be wirelessly sent to larger desktop screens and wireless TVs for the whole family to enjoy, and there are even games that let two people play on the same iPad screen. For modern entertainment, few single products can match the iPad.

Entertainment and home-based activities are also widely covered in the App Store. You name the subject, and a solution will be available. From planning a garden to building an inventory of your home contents to sharing special moments and enjoying media, the App Store builds on the wealth of functionality already present in the iPad and takes its flexibility to a whole new level.

We mentioned the lounge coffee table at the start, and Newsstand takes us full circle thanks to its ability to deliver hundreds of popular magazine titles to your iPad as soon as each issue is released. Many of the titles feel like real paper magazines, and some even include multimedia content to immerse you deeper into the experience. This, along with the latest iBooks solution, is another feature that entire families can enjoy together. There are countless other examples where an iPad can be useful and enjoyable in the home, and over time the benefits will become clear. Many people see computers as devices that stop people interacting, but the iPad proves that digital devices can be a source of enjoyment, organisation and even bring families together to enjoy shared experiences. In fact, to call an iPad a computer is probably ignoring what it really is, because it often feels so natural to use that anyone can create and gain enjoyment from the experience. It is a device that everyone can enjoy, no matter what age they are, and one that truly defines modern computing.

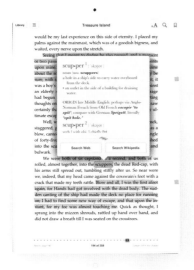

*Having an iPad at home could be even more convenient than a laptop or desktop PC*

# 5 top tips for using your iPad in the home

## 1 Lose the wires
An iPad is mobile by default, so take some time to check out the wireless solutions that are available to you. Whether it is for printing, playing games or watching movies, you can do all of this without any wires at all.

## 2 Innovative solutions
There are accessories available that will let you store and charge your iPad from one convenient location. Whether you use a desktop cradle or even a picture frame-style solution, look for something that will suit the whole family.

## 3 Think iPad first
Most computing tasks you need to undertake in the home will be simple, so you should think about the iPad before picking up a laptop or going to your desktop computer. It will likely be much quicker and more convenient to use.

## 4 Be creative
Remember that you can create on an iPad. Whether you need to make an inventory of your home or plan a new garden, there are apps available that will help you to improve your home life, not just supplement it.

## 5 Children will benefit
There are countless books and apps available for the iPad that will help children to learn and have fun. iBooks has now been updated (page 128) for a better browsing experience and connectivity with the cloud.

# On the go

## You can use an iPad in its entirety no matter where you are or what you need to do

The new iPads are capable of becoming the ultimate road warrior, not to mention a tool that will let you leave the laptop on your desk. The 3G version lets you connect anywhere a mobile data signal is present, and on some networks it is possible to achieve speeds in excess of what is available in the office using Wi-Fi. This frees up the iPad and the user to work and play no matter where they are, and the extra portability makes it ideal for long train journeys and the daily commute. Even without a valid data connection, the battery life of the iPad makes it ideal for watching films during a long plane journey, or even for keeping the kids amused when driving.

For more serious uses, there are many navigation solutions that work on the iPad, such as the new Maps app, which can turn it into the ultimate in-car solution. The larger screen makes checking your route safer, and with suitable mounting accessories you could dispense with your car stereo, standalone sat nav and other driving-related devices. The Maps app can work as a real-time moving map when taking long walks or exploring the countryside, and all of this will work when planning journeys and even booking hotels and flights for your next holiday.

The camera on the new iPad should not be ignored, because it is well specified and capable of capturing some quality snaps that can be immediately shared via social networks for fun, or via email for more serious purposes. Whether you need to capture and store a receipt or take a quick video of your children enjoying themselves, you can do all this with the iPad and upload the results to YouTube in double-quick time. The Twitter and Facebook integration in iOS 6 is so deeply embedded now that sharing anything you capture on your iPad or simply sharing your thoughts are just a few taps away.

*As you will have come to expect by now, the iPad is ideal for using while on the move*

iCloud is vital to a lot of what you will do on the iPad, and every photo you take will be stored immediately in your Photo Stream for accessing from other devices later. Your documents can be worked on and saved at any time, and as you would expect, you can email, instant message and make contact with others whenever you need to. The options available to communicate with others are varied, and put a connected iPad on a par with a smartphone, only with a larger screen and better battery life.

Your entire music library can be carried with you and shared using a speaker dock or wirelessly via connected stereo systems, and when you seriously think about what a laptop will do for you when you are travelling – even high-end models – it soon becomes clear that an iPad can do most

of the same tasks in a much more efficient manner. An iPad offers class-leading battery performance, is extremely portable, and can effectively become a replacement laptop with accessories such as a keyboard, which lets you work with it in exactly same way you would normally interact with a laptop. For the vast majority of users, an iPad is actually more convenient, and will let them enjoy entertainment more easily and work more efficiently. There are very few tasks that a laptop is better at than an iPad, apart from specialist needs for business.

Even non-3G iPads can be used when mobile with the addition of a Mi-Fi style device, which lets the user use a mobile broadband connection in the same way a 3G enabled iPad can. It can actually be more beneficial, because the Mi-Fi can be used with other devices such as smartphones and multiple devices at the same time, so your options are varied, and can be changed to suit your particular needs. Is there a better product to carry with you on business trips, holidays or anywhere else? Probably not.

## "Even non-3G iPads can be connected to 3G broadbands via a Mi-Fi device"

*The iPad is ideal for route finding and navigation-related tasks*

# 5 top tips for using your iPad on the go

## 1 3G without 3G
You can still use a 3G broadband connection via a Mi-Fi device if your iPad does not include a SIM card slot. In some ways this can be cheaper and more flexible, because you can use it for other devices as well.

## 2 Keep it safe
You should always carry your iPad in a suitable case. When travelling anywhere, it makes sense to protect it and even disguise it as something else. iPads, like most tablets, often do not survive drops onto hard surfaces.

## 3 In the car
There are mounts available for iPads that let them work in your car. You will need to spend time finding the right solution, but with some thought you could turn your iPad into the ultimate in-car entertainment system.

## 4 Think about power
Think about your power requirements if you are travelling for a few days. iPads don't charge well via USB from laptops etc, so make sure that you are carrying the right charger and that it will keep the iPad running for extended periods of time.

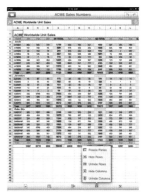

## 5 Compatibility
If you are working on the move, ensure that you are using apps that can create documents in formats that are readable by others. Remember that many people still require Microsoft Office-formatted documents, but there are many iPad apps (like iWork) that support these.

# Settings

Explore the inner workings of your iPad as we guide you through some of its more important enhancements and changes that you will need

## Use it to:

- **Manage notifications**
Customise the apps you want to send you notifications

- **Manage your iCloud**
Get to grips with Photo Stream and more

- **Back up your iPad**
Choose when to back up your device to iCloud

- **Wireless updates**
Check if your iOS is up to date or get a wireless update

- **Find My iPad**
Locate your device on a map and remotely lock or erase it

- **Enable restrictions**
Passcode protect your device and set restrictions on apps

- **Utilise Location Services**
Determine which apps source info based on your location

*Fig 1 (main image): Swipe down from the top of any screen to view your Notification Center*

*Fig 2 (top left): Tap on an app in the list and you can determine how it conducts on-screen alerts*

*Fig 3 (bottom left): Tap Notifications to view the list of apps in your Center. Tap Edit to make changes*

# Take control of your iPad

Manage app notifications, get to grips with iCloud and much more in Settings

## Manage your notifications

Your iPad sends you all kinds of notifications – new emails, text messages, friend requests and app alerts – and with Notification Center, you can keep track of them, all in one convenient location.

Just swipe down from the top of any screen to enter Notification Center and view the complete list of all your recent notifications (see Fig 1). New notifications will also appear briefly at the top of your screen without interrupting what you're doing, and the Lock screen displays notifications so you can act on them with just one swipe.

To tailor Notification Center to your own specific needs, launch the Settings app and then tap on the Notifications section from the main Settings list. The main screen presents a list of apps that are in your Notification Center and a list of those that are not (Fig 3). By tapping the Edit button in the top-right corner you can move apps between lists and change the order of how the apps appear in Notification Center. Do Not Disturb will stop notifications appearing on your screen, but they will still come through - it's perfect for when you're asleep.

To determine how your iPad receives alerts, tap on an app in the list and you can set the style of alert (how and where it will appear) and also whether or not it will flash up on your Lock screen (Fig 2).

*Fig 1: You can select which apps use iCloud by tapping on the iCloud section of the Settings app and moving the sliders to the On position*

# "Perhaps the best example of iCloud in effect is through Photo Stream"

## Your personal iCloud

Apple's iCloud service is free to use and stores your music, photos, documents and more, and wirelessly pushes them to all of your iOS devices without you having to manually transfer files. Most of Apple's built-in iPad apps use iCloud in some form to sync data – such as contacts, calendars and reminders across devices. Perhaps the best example of iCloud in effect is through Photo Stream, as shown in Fig 2 below. What this means is any photos you take on your iPhone will be automatically – and wirelessly – pushed to your iPad.

You can determine which apps use iCloud by launching your Settings app and then tapping iCloud. Move the sliders of the apps you wish to benefit from iCloud to On and the changes will be immediate (Fig 1).

Your iCloud account also comes with 5GB of free storage. To check how much free space you have, tap on the 'Storage & Backup' option (Fig 3, below). To see how much of your free storage your apps use, tap on the 'Manage Storage' option. You can delete data by tapping on an app and selecting the 'Edit' button in the top right.

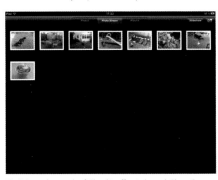

*Fig 2: A good example of iCloud in effect is through Photo Stream – take a picture on your iPhone and it will appear on your iPad*

*Fig 3: You can see how much of your free 5GB allocation you are using by tapping on Storage & Backup>Manage Storage*

## Buy more storage

If the free 5GB allocation isn't sufficient, you can buy more

### 1: Go to iCloud Settings

Launch your Settings app and then tap on the iCloud section in the list.

### 2: Tap on Storage & Backup

From the main iCloud settings screen, tap on the Storage & Backup option.

### 3: Tap on Buy More Storage

Now tap Buy More Storage and review the three additional space options.

### 4: Purchase space

Tap on one of the options and then Buy. Make the most of your extra space!

# Settings

## Your iCloud account
Your iCloud account is tied in with your iTunes account that you have set up on your device to purchase media and apps

## Compatible apps
All of the apps that incorporate iCloud will be presented in a list. Move the sliders to the On position to activate their iCloud features

## Available storage
Tap on the Storage & Backup option to review how much of your cloud you are using and buy more space if necessary

## Delete Accounts
If you wish to delete your iCloud account and start afresh then the Delete Account option is available on the main screen

## Back up your iPad
As you undoubtedly have all sorts of important stuff on your iPad, iCloud will provide sound peace of mind by automatically backing up your device daily over Wi-Fi when your device is connected to a power source. Once you plug it in all of your apps, media and files are backed up quickly.

When you set up a new iPad or need to restore the information on one you already have, iCloud does all the heavy lifting for you. Just connect your device to Wi-Fi, enter your Apple ID and your personal data, along with purchased music, TV shows and books, and apps will magically appear on your device. To activate this service, launch your Settings app and then tap on the iCloud section. Then tap on the Storage & Backup option and ensure that the slider under 'iCloud Backup' is moved to the all-important On position (see Fig 1). All of your data will be automatically backed up when your iPad is plugged in, locked and connected to a Wi-Fi network.

You can also override the process and instruct your iPad to back up to iCloud immediately by tapping 'Back Up Now' at the bottom of Storage & Backup (Fig 2).

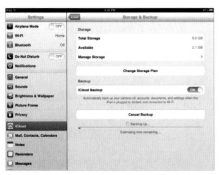

*Fig 1: Go to the Storage & Backup section in the iCloud settings to activate the auto-backup feature*

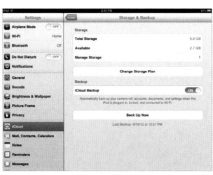

*Fig 2: To back up your data instantly, tap on the Back Up Now option and the process will take place immediately*

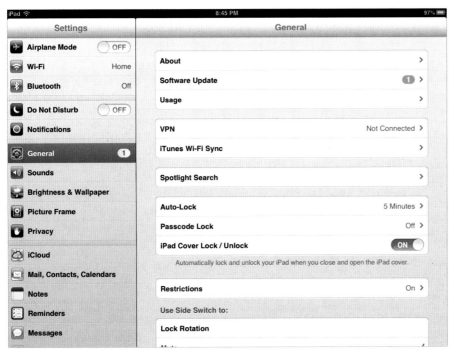

Fig 1: Tap on the General section in the Settings app and you will see the Software Update option at the top of the page. The '1' shows that we have got one update waiting. Tap it and your iPad will update – as long as you're connected to Wi-Fi

# "If a new update is detected then you can opt to download and install it"

## Wireless software updates

You no longer need a computer to own an iPad; you can now activate and set up your device wirelessly, straight out of the box and download free iOS software updates directly on your iPad.

What's more, rather than tie your iPad up by wirelessly downloading huge hulking data files to update the system, only the required elements will be updated and installed, making it quick and easy to keep your iPad's software up to date. If your iPad's operating system is out of date and there is a new, free

update available then you will be notified via a small red alert that appears next to your Settings app icon. When this occurs, launch your Settings app and then tap on the General section in the settings list (Fig 1). At the top of this page will be an option called Software Update – tap this option and your device will start scanning for new updates, provided it is connected to a Wi-Fi network (Fig 2). If a new update is detected then you can opt to download and install it on your device (Fig 3). This may take a few minutes and your device will refresh when the process is complete.

Fig 2: Tap on the Software Update option and your device will start scanning to see if new updates are available

Fig 3: If an iOS update is found, you will have the choice to download and install it

## Sync without a PC
Instantly sync your multimedia to your iPad

### 1: Go to General settings
Launch your Settings app and then tap on the General section.

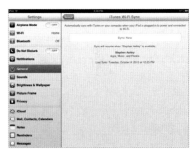

### 2: Activate Wi-Fi Sync
With your iPad connected to a power source and Wi-Fi, tap iTunes Wi-Fi Sync.

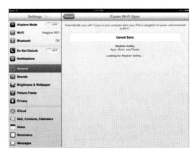

### 3: Sync now
Tap Sync Now and your multimedia will be synced between devices.

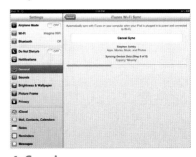

### 4: Syncing process
The syncing process may take a few minutes. Do not disconnect your device.

# Set shortcuts

## Enable keyboard shortcuts to make iPad typing easy

### 1: Go to Keyboard section

Launch your Settings app and then tap on General and Keyboard.

### 2: Enable shortcuts

Move the shortcut sliders to 'On' to enable the various features.

### 3: Adding shortcuts

To start adding in your own shortcuts, tap on Add New Shortcut.

### 4: Creating shortcuts

Type in a word or phrase followed by the shortcut that you wish to use.

## Syncing iTunes

Tapping the Sync Now option will ensure all of your purchased iTunes content is synced between your iPad and computer

## Cancel sync

If the process is taking too long and you need to abort then you can tap on the Cancel Sync button to halt the process

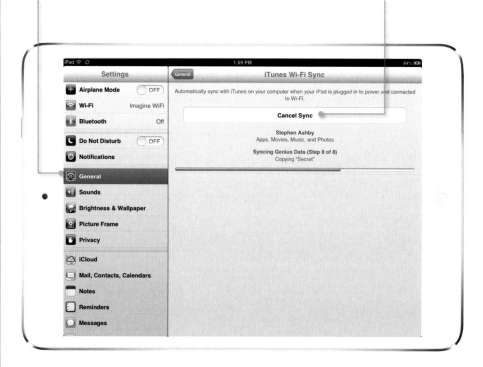

## Find My iPad

As your iPad is packed full of personal data, a natural sense of panic will set in if, for some reason, you happen to misplace it. But try not to worry too much because iCloud has it covered. By activating the Find My iPad feature in the Settings app under iCloud (slide the slider to 'On'), you will be able to locate your device on a map, which may help you pinpoint its location and retrieve it, or send a message to whoever finds it. And, if necessary, you can remotely lock your device to prevent others from gaining access or erase the contents altogether.

To use this feature you will need to open up the iCloud section of Settings and switch the slider to the On position next to Find My iPhone. You can also download the Find My iPhone app, which, when launched, will pinpoint your device on a map and enable you to send a message to it, or remote lock or erase the contents (Fig 2).

Obviously you can't use this app on a device that is missing, so you can either download it for another iOS device to find the missing iPad or even log onto www.icloud.com on your desktop Mac or PC and then use the app through your computer.

*Fig 1: Download the free Find My iPhone app from the App Store to track down all your devices*

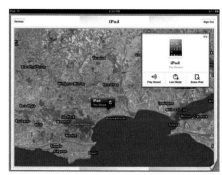

*Fig 2: Launch the app to locate your missing device on a map and remotely lock the device or erase the contents*

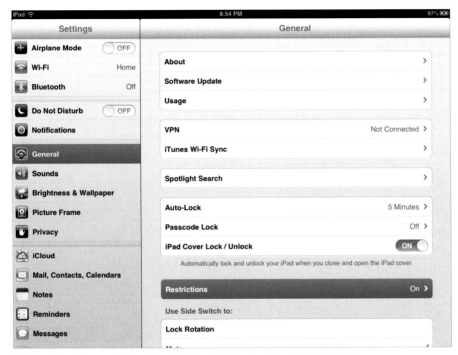

Fig 1: To enable restrictions, go to Settings>General and tap on Restrictions to get imposing rules and codes

## Set a passcode
Secure your device with a cryptic code

### 1: Go to General settings
Launch your Settings app and then tap on the General section.

### 2: Choose Passcode Lock
Tap on Passcode Lock and then turn the feature on using the top option.

### 3: Turn off Simple Passcode
Turn the Simple Passcode option to the Off position and enter your passcode.

## Enable restrictions

As you have invested quite a significant sum of money on your iPad and the various apps and iTunes media content on it, you will naturally want to impose restrictions on who can access your material. Likewise, if your device is shared throughout the family then enabling restrictions will mean that inappropriate material cannot be accessed through the device and that expensive apps can't be purchased by accident.

To start enabling restrictions, go to the General settings section and then tap on Restrictions (see Fig 1 above). By tapping the 'Enable Restrictions' option at the top of the page, you will first be required to enter a four-digit passcode. Do so and then move the sliders to the On position of the apps that may be accessed (Fig 2) and then scroll down and review the list of allowed content.

To impose greater restrictions, go back to the General page and tap on 'Passcode Lock'. This code will have to be entered every time you unlock your device. If you wish to enable a more secure password then move the Simple Passcode slider to Off and then you'll be able to use your full keyboard to enter a more secure password (Fig 3).

## "Enabling restrictions will mean that inappropriate material cannot be accessed"

Fig 2: Review the page of restrictions and allowed content and tailor them to your own specific needs and parental requirements

Fig 3: To make a more secure password, go to Passcode Lock and turn the Simple Passcode option off

### 4: Secure passcoding
You can now use your entire iPad keyboard to create a more secure code.

# Change Wallpaper

## Why not brighten up your iPad Home and Lock screens?

## 1: Find your options
Launch your Settings app and then tap on the Brightness & Wallpaper section.

## 2: Tap on Wallpaper
Tap on either the Lock or Home screen image under the Wallpaper section.

## 3: Pick a background
You can use an existing wallpaper or choose one of your own photos.

## 4: Set wallpaper
To set one, open it and choose either Set Lock Screen or Set Home Screen.

## Simple Passcode
By default this is set to a simple four-digit code, but by turning this function off you can set something much more cryptic

## Erase Data
For the more security conscious, you can turn on the option to erase the data on your iPad if the code is entered incorrectly ten times

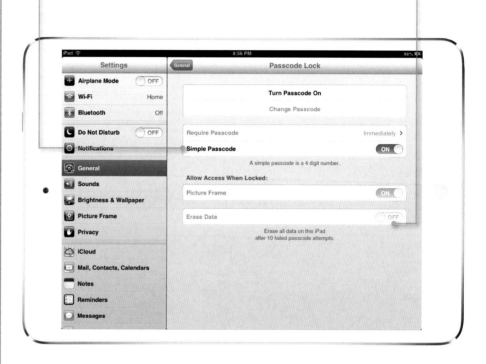

## Set up Location Services
Location Services allows location-dependent apps and websites (including Maps, Camera, and Safari) to use information from cellular, Wi-Fi and Global Position System (GPS) networks to determine your location. For example, an app might use your location and location search query to help you find nearby amenities or your device may set its time zone automatically based on your current location.

Apps that use Location Services will often ask to use your location when you first launch them, but you can also determine which apps are granted such privileges by tapping on the Location Services option in the Privacy section of Settings. Here you will be presented with a list of apps that use location data and can manually turn them on or off, according to your preference (Fig 1). You can also review and set various system services, by tapping on the option at the bottom of the screen, which enables more general settings to be applied.

The Location Services section in Settings will also explain what the various arrows at the top of your iPad display mean when an app is currently using your location or a geo-fence (a virtual perimeter around a location – as used by apps such as Reminders) is in effect (Fig 2).

*Fig 1: The System Services option enables you to grant your iPad permission to change the time zone based on your location*

*Fig 2: The Location Services section provides great descriptions of the different coloured arrows you'll come across*

## Set up iPad VPN

Virtual Private Networks (VPN) are often used within organisations and companies to allow you to communicate private information securely over a public network. You may need to configure VPN, for example, to access your work email on multiple iOS devices, like your iPhone and iPad.

VPN works over both Wi-Fi and cellular data network connections and to configure a VPN you must go to the General section of your Settings app and then tap on the VPN section (Fig 1). Here you can simply switch the slider to On (Fig 2); you might need to ask your network administrator which settings to use. In most cases, if you've set up a similar VPN on your computer, you can use the same VPN settings for your iOS device (Fig 3).

When you have created a VPN configuration, the option to turn VPN on or off will appear in the list to the left of the main settings screen and when you are connected using VPN, the VPN icon will be visible in the status bar at the top of your iPad's Home screen.

If you are having trouble connecting to your VPN connection, or if you see an alert that says 'Shared Secret is missing,' then your VPN settings may be incorrect or incomplete, so go over the steps to confirm that you have configured it properly. If you have any questions about what your VPN settings are or what your Shared Secret key is, you will need to contact your network administrator or the IT Department of your company as they are the best people to help you.

# Set a picture frame
## How to turn your iPad into a digital photo frame

### 1: Toggle settings
Go to Picture Frame in Settings to be presented with various options.

### 2: Set duration
Next, set how long you want each photo displayed for.

### 3: Choose images
You can opt to display all available images or just a select few.

### 4: Watch slideshow
Tap the flower icon from the lock screen to turn your device into a photo frame.

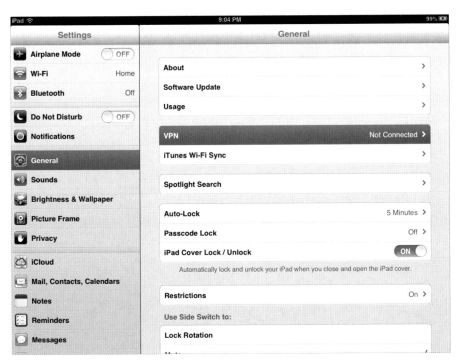

*Fig 1: To start setting up a VPN, tap on the General section in Settings and then tap on the Network option*

*Fig 2: You will be asked to enter details as soon as you turn the feature on. You will need to get these from your network provider*

*Fig 3: Once you have entered the details required to set up VPN, tap Save and an icon in your status bar will indicate connection*

# App Store

Your gateway to a rich source of apps is via the intuitive App Store app. We show you how it works

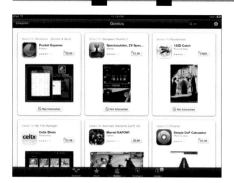

Fig 1 (top): Turning on Genius is akin to having your very own personal app shopper…

Fig 2 (bottom-left): Searching by category allows you to scour the app areas that interest you

Fig 3 (main image): The Featured section of the App Store is an eye-catching display of the greatest and latest apps

## Use it to:

- **Store navigation**
  You can easily find exciting new content.

- **Search smartly**
  Find exactly what you want by filtering.

- **Purchase apps**
  Buy new apps and media quickly and easily.

- **Gift an app**
  Send someone an app that they need as a gift.

- **Utilise Genius**
  Get instant recommendations based on your other applications.

- **Make use of iCloud**
  Re-download your past.

# Shopping for apps

## The App Store app is packed full of features to help you find the latest and greatest apps for your iPad

### Navigating the App Store

The first thing that you'll notice when you initially launch the App Store is how exciting it looks. You will be directed to the Featured section by default and this is the vibrant shop window that regularly showcases the most exciting apps to be released in recent weeks. Within this section of the App Store are further places to delve into and explore, such as What's Hot and New & Noteworthy (Fig 3, above). The latter lets you view the most up-to-date additions, and buttons along the top let you filter these results by category. You can also navigate to other sections using the labelled buttons at the bottom of the screen. These include Genius (Fig 1), which, when activated, will source and recommend apps based on what's currently on your iPad, and Charts that allows you to see the 200 most popular apps of the hour.

If you are looking for something specific then you can enter key words into the Search field or browse specific categories from the top of the page (Fig 2), which can help to narrow down what you're looking for. This includes the Newsstand area, which allows you to download magazines and newspapers to a special section of your iPad.

Fig 1: Start typing words into the Search field and suggestions will start coming thick and fast

# "It may seem like an overly populated interface, but it's easy to master"

## Searching the App Store

Considering that the shelves of the App Store have swelled to over 700,000 apps, being able to find what you need quickly is of the utmost importance. It's just as well, then, that there is an intuitive search engine on hand to help. If you know the name of the app you're looking for, then enter it into the Search field. As you type, matches will instantly start being made (Fig 1). If you see what you want in the list of suggestions, then just tap on it to instantly go to that page. If you're not totally sure of what you're looking for, then there are plenty of handy points to steer you in the right direction. The Featured section is a good starting point as it showcases the latest eye-catching apps (Fig 2). From there, you can use the Charts button at the bottom of the screen to see what's popular among worldwide users, or begin searching in an area of interest, such as Music or Photo & Video using the category buttons at the top.

You can also browse by the What's Hot and New & Noteworthy categories that are accessible from the page (Fig 3). The latter presents recently updated apps, those that are getting a lot of press coverage, or apps that are just brand new to the Store.

Fig 2: The Featured section of the App Store is a great starting point to go in search of new apps for your iPad

Fig 3: Viewing New and Noteworthy is a great way to see what's hot on the app store

## Redeem a gift card
### How to top up your Store credit with codes

### 1: Go to Featured
Tap on the Featured icon at the bottom of the screen.

### 2: Scroll down
Scroll down to the bottom of the page and tap Redeem.

### 3: Enter code
Enter the redeem code you have been given into the text box.

### 4: Download product
Your app will now be downloaded or your credit will be topped up.

**Buying**
Tap on the price of a product to start the purchase and download process. Log in and ensure you have credit in your account

**Search**
Enter key words into the search field to help you find apps featured within the store

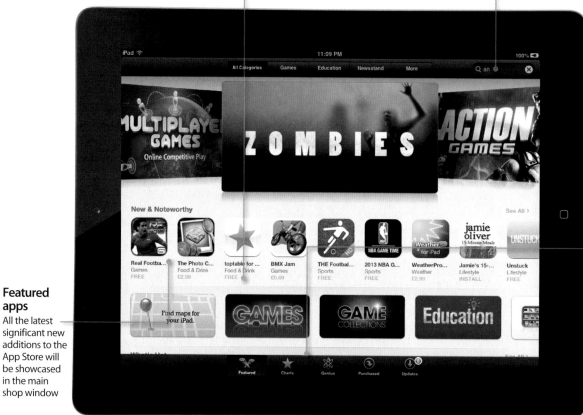

**Featured apps**
All the latest significant new additions to the App Store will be showcased in the main shop window

**Sections**
You will be able to access specific stores for Charts, Genius recommendations and more at the bottom of the screen

## Purchasing apps

Being the only source of gaining apps for your iPad, the App Store is, as you would expect, a quick and easy way to shop for new apps – and purchasing them really couldn't be simpler. You will already be logged in to the App Store with your registered Apple ID, which should have your billing details attached. If you haven't already added the

details of a valid credit or debit card for your app charge to be taken from, then tap on the Featured page at the App Store, scroll down to the bottom and tap on your Apple ID.

Select View Apple ID from the menu and then tap on the Payment Information option (Fig 1). You can now select a card type and enter all of the required information so that all app purchases will be made using that card.

Now you can tap on the price of an app (Fig 2) and then complete the purchase by simply entering your Apple ID password.

You will still need to enter your Apple ID password when downloading free apps (Fig 3), but the good news is that you don't have to assign a credit or debit card to do so. You can just sign in and the app will be downloaded straight away.

*Fig 1: Tap on your Apple ID and then tap Payment Information to assign a credit or debit card to your account*

*Fig 2: Tap on the price of an app to commence the purchasing process*

*Fig 3: You will need to sign in using your Apple ID before you can confirm transactions*

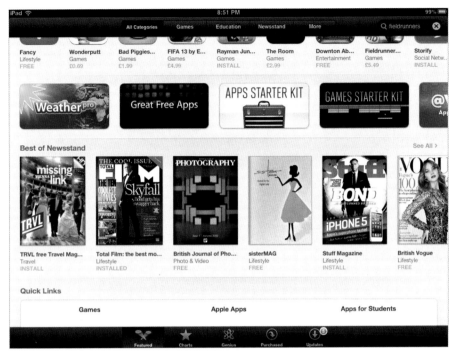

*Fig 1: Scroll down in the Featured section and you'll see a selection of the best newspapers and magazines for your iPad.*

# "You can get your favourite magazines and newspapers delivered to your iPad"

## Newsstand

When Apple launched iOS 5 last year, they included a brand new app with the system, called Newsstand. This allows users to download magazines and newspapers to their devices and see them all appear in a special folder on your home screen. Of course, this is perfect if you subscribe to a lot of magazines, or buy a newspaper every day, as you can get your news fix delivered to your iPad automatically. New editions of your chosen subscription will be downloaded even when your iPad is locked overnight.

There is a specific section of the App Store dedicated to these apps, and if you scroll down to the bottom of the Featured page you will see some of the best magazines and newspapers available. When you find one you like, tap to install the free app on your device, and from inside that app you will be able to browse the digital editions of the title and decide which ones to buy and download. Some magazines will simply be digital representations of a page, while others will use all the features of the iPad to offer a complete multi-media experience.

*Fig 2: You can get a brief description and preview of the latest edition in the app information page*

*Fig 3: The app is free, and you can download issues of your favourite magazine from within them for a small price*

## Update an app
Ensure you have the latest version of your favourite apps

### 1: Go to the App Store
First of all, launch the App Store app on your beloved iPad.

### 2: Tap on Updates
Tap on the Updates tab at the bottom of the screen.

### 3: Find an app
Scroll the list for an app to update or tap Update All.

### 4: Tap Update
Tap on the Update button and the new version will begin installing.

# Review & rate apps
## Provide a critique for other users

### 1: Go to app page
Tap the app you want to review to see its information appear.

### 2: Choose Ratings
From the options under the app's icon, tap Ratings and Reviews.

### 3: Tap the stars
Tap the stars to leave an individual rating for the app, 5 being the best app.

### 4: Write a review
Tap the Write a Review link and then write and submit a review.

## Update All
If you have numerous apps with free updates available, tap on the Update All button in the top-left corner of the screen

## Update info
Apps with updates listed in the Updates section of the App Store provide lists of all of the enhancements made to the latest version

## Tell a friend about an app
The App Store has a built-in sharing interface that lets you share great apps with your friends so that they too can experience them and even compete against you via Game Center. And, in iOS 6, there are even more ways to share with your friends from inside the App store. To tell a friend about an app, all you have to do is go to the app's info page, which you do by tapping on the name of the app in the App Store (Fig 1). Then, in the top-right corner, you will see a Sharing button. Tap this and you'll have a range of options for sharing the app with your contacts.

Whether you choose Facebook, Twitter, iMessage or email, this is a great way to spread instant app awareness and ensure that your friends are stocking up with the apps that you're playing so that you can enjoy online multiplayer playing experiences and compete for the highest score in the online leaderboards – all of which can be accessed via Game Center (which we shall get to, in details, later). Plus, with Twitter and Facebook support, you can tell groups of friends and followers about an app quickly and easily – perfect for when you find an app you know your followers will love.

*Fig 1: Go to the App Store and tap on an individual app to access its information page*

*Fig 2: Tap the Sharing button and you'll have a number of sharing options available to you to spread the word fast*

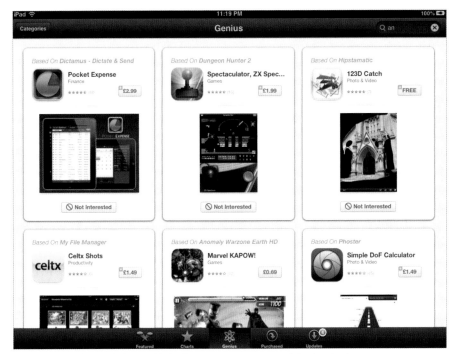

Fig 1: Tap the Genius button at the bottom of the App Store screen to access recommendations based on the apps you own

# "You can clearly see the app that inspired the recommendation"

## Genius

Like with iTunes, in which the Genius feature can be utilised to get song recommendations based on the music in your library and create playlists that group together similar-sounding songs, the App Store too has its own little Genius at work.

While in the App Store, tap the Genius button at the bottom of the window and you'll be taken to a screen full of Genius recommendations based on the apps that you have downloaded previously (Fig 1). The layout of this page is simple to digest as you can clearly see the app that inspired the recommendation. Purchase the

recommended app straight from the Genius page or register that you are not interested by tapping the button underneath the recommendation. If you then tap on the More arrow then you can scroll through even more possibilities (Fig 2).

You can also use the Categories button in the top-left corner of the screen to narrow down the results of your Genius results into specific kinds of apps (Fig 3). So, if you love games and have bought several, you can quickly see what Apple recommends for you, without apps from other categories like Productivity or Finance getting in the way of what you're interested in.

Fig 2: To view more, simply scroll down to see more suggested apps

Fig 3: Use the Categories button in the top-left to narrow down the results.

## Removing an app
How to delete an app from your iPad

### 1: Go to the page
Go to the Home screen page where the app is situated.

### 2: Press and hold
Press and hold down on the app icon until it shakes.

### 3: Tap the cross
Tap on the 'X' next to the app you wish to remove it.

### 4: Confirm choice
When the confirmation message appears, tap on Delete.

# Re-download an app

Ensure past purchases
are always close at hand

## 1: Go to Purchased

Once in the App Store, tap Purchased at
the bottom of the screen.

## 2: Tap Not On This iPad

Now tap on the Not On This iPad tab at
the top of the page.

## 3: Tap cloud icon

An iCloud icon will be visible next to
your previous purchases. Tap on one.

## 4: Instant download

You no longer need to sign in before
your app downloads. It's now instant.

## Re-download apps

To re-download past purchases that are Not
On This iPad, tap the tab at the top of the
Purchased section

## iCloud at work

Your purchases are backed up to your
iCloud, so tap on the cloud icon to
re-download the apps

## Automatic downloads

With iCloud, every purchase you make
through iTunes and the App Store (including
the iBooks Store) will be written in your own
cloud, so a record is also kept up to date and
you'll always be able to re-download any
purchase you have ever made. With iCloud,
you can also get your downloads pushed to all
of your other iOS devices wirelessly, too.

This feature, known as Automatic
Downloads, has to be activated in Settings
before it kicks in, so launch the app and then
tap on the iTunes & App Stores category in the
left-hand list (Fig 1). Automatic Downloads are
shown on the right.

Move the slider of the Apps category to the
On position to ensure that any purchases
(including free downloads) that you have
made on other devices will now automatically
be downloaded to your iPad.

Apps that aren't compatible with iPad
won't be downloaded, but universal apps that
you've downloaded on your iPhone will be
pushed to your iPad too, saving you the extra
time and hassle of going back to the App
Store on your iPad and downloading the same
app again (Fig 2). This can save your workload
by a lot. See the tutorial to the left for a step-
by-step guide to this useful function in the
new App Store.

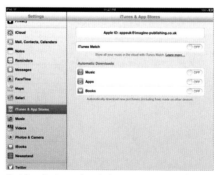

*Fig 1: Go to Settings and tap the Store section to activate the
Automatic Downloads feature*

*Fig 2: You can now get all content purchased on other devices
pushed to your iPad*

*Fig 1: Press and hold on an app then drag it over another app to create a folder*

# "There is a system in place that allows you to easily manage your apps"

## Manage your apps

With so many apps, thousands of which are free to download, available from the App Store, it's inevitable that the multiple Home screens of your iPad will become congested with app icons. Thankfully, there is a system in place that allows you to easily manage them and move them into neat little folders.

To create a folder, press and hold on an app icon until the screen shakes and small 'X' icons appear next to each app. Press and hold on an app and then drag it on top of another app icon to create a folder (Fig 1). The app you move and the app you drag the other

icon onto will then be placed into the folder and you can repeat the process to drag more apps into the same folder or create different ones. The folder will be titled in accordance with the apps that you place in it, but you can rename the folders and call them what you want by tapping the 'X' next to the title bar and then using the keyboard to type in the new name (Fig 2). When you have finished organising your apps, press the Home button and the apps will be locked into place. Up to 20 apps can be stored in folders, which is great for keeping your Home screens neat and tidy (Fig 3).

*Fig 2: You can easily rename the folders by tapping the 'X' to the right of the default title*

*Fig 3: Folders can help to keep your Home screens neat and tidy*

## Customer services
### What to do if you have an app problem

### 1: Go to info page
Tap the name of the app in the App Store to access its info page.

### 2: Find App Support
Tap Ratings and Reviews and you'll see an App Support button. Tap it now.

### 3: Get support
You will be taken to the developer site where you can email your queries.

### 4: Tap an email
Tap on the customer services email address to send your query from the app.

# iTunes

Explore the world's premier digital entertainment superstore on your iPad and get all of the hottest new albums, movies and more beamed directly to your device

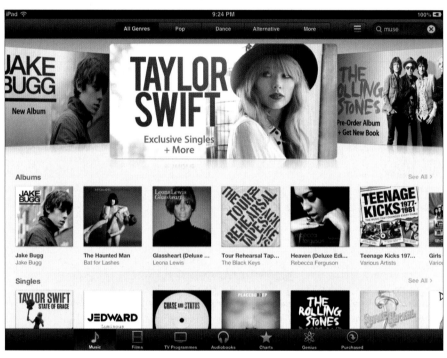

## Use it to:

- **Store navigation**
  Sections make it easy to find new content and great deals.

- **Search smartly**
  Find what you want by entering keywords.

- **Purchase items**
  Buying new music and movies is a painless process.

- **Gift an item**
  Send a gift to loved ones.

- **Make use of Genius**
  Get artist recommendations and create smart playlists.

- **Utilise iTunes U**
  Get access to a wealth of free study materials.

- **Get iTunes in the Cloud**
  Get instant access to all of your music.

*Fig 1 (top left): See what's currently hot with other shoppers by tapping Charts at the bottom*

*Fig 2 (bottom left): Use the buttons at the bottom of the window to access Store sections*

*Fig 3 (main image): The Featured window of the iTunes app showcases the very latest music*

# Explore iTunes

Navigate the expansive iTunes Store on your iPad with the sleek and intuitive iTunes app

### iTunes Categories

The world's premier online entertainment store will already be familiar to millions, and in app form it is easier than ever to purchase and download music, movies and TV shows. When you launch the app you'll be taken straight to the Featured section of the store that showcases all of the latest additions to the music library (see Fig 3). You can tap on any banner at the top of the screen to be taken to the info page of the respective album or scroll down to the Album and Singles sections that have new releases that you may be interested in. To see what's currently hot, tap the Charts button at the bottom of the screen (Fig 1).

You can search for specific artists or albums by entering text into the search field, and explore much more of what the iTunes Store has to offer by tapping the other buttons at the bottom of the window (Fig 2).

Here you will see links to the Films and TV Programmes sections, as well as a specific place to go for Audio books, and your previously purchased content, which can be instantly downloaded again for free. Much of this content requires you to have credit in your Apple account in order to purchase content. There is so much to explore that you're better off just exploring it on your own and discovering its many delights for yourself.

*Fig 1: You can tap the button in the top-right to see a list of all the items you've previewed instantly*

## iTunes Previews

For a long time now, you've been able to preview items in the iTunes Store to get a taste of what you're buying before you download it. In iOS 6, however, these previews have been extended, and you can also keep track of what it is you've been considering at any time.

Before iOS 6 you could preview songs for around 30 seconds, and watch trailers for movies and TV shows that interested you within the store. Now, that preview length has been increased to one and a half minutes for songs, giving you a much better idea of what you're getting. These previews also continue to play while you navigate around the store, whereas before they would stop if you moved to a different album or artist. A controller appears in the top-right, allowing you to stop the preview, or quickly buy the song if you decide to do so.

As well as this, a small button on the right of the categories bar at the top of the screen offers you the ability to track all the previews you have viewed over time. They're sorted by date, and the list includes every media type, including movie trailers and TV show clips. It's the perfect 'try before you buy' system, and it's incredibly easy to use on the iPad.

## "Previews offer the perfect 'try before you buy' system on your iPad"

*Fig 2: The new preview controller will sit in the top-right, over everything on-screen, so you can quickly buy the song*

*Fig 3: Every preview you choose will be added to the list, including movie trailers and clips from TV shows*

## Download tracks
How to purchase and download your prize finds

### 1: Find item
Search iTunes for a song, an album or an audiobook and then tap on it.

### 2: Tap the price
Tap on the price of the item and then tap again when it says Buy.

### 3: Download
It will be added to your downloads and you can check its progress.

### 4: Tap Purchased
Tap on the Purchased tab and you'll be able to play the track in your Music app.

## Featured music
All the latest significant new additions to the iTunes Store will be showcased in the main shop window

## Search
Enter key words into the search field to find specific artists and songs featured within the store

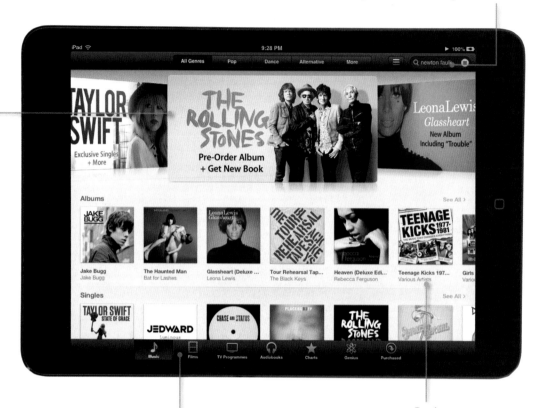

## Sections
You will be able to access specific stores for Music, Films, TV Programmes and Audio books at the bottom of the screen

## Buying
Tap on the price of a product to start the purchase and download process. You must be logged in with credit in your account

## iTunes U

As well as music and entertainment, the iTunes app also provides a gateway into education with an ever-expanding catalogue of resource material and study aids to assist in a wide range of topics. In fact, so popular has the service proved that Apple has recently released a dedicated standalone iTunes U app (see Fig 1). When you have installed the app, the interface will be near identical to the iBooks and Newsstand interfaces in that you have rows of shelves to store your downloaded materials and a special, dedicated section of the App Store that is instantly accessible via the Catalog button in the top-left. Tap on this to browse for learning tools to download. When you find a suitable course, tap on 'Get Course' and your materials will be downloaded for free (Fig 2) and take up residence on your shelves back in the main window. From there you can simply tap on a course to view it, and a neat new interface will let you navigate your way through it and apply your own notes (Fig 3) as and where you need to. iTunes U resources aren't available directly through iTunes, but the interface is almost identical.

*Fig 1: Search for iTunes U on the App Store or tap the iTunes U category in your iTunes app to be taken to the download page*

*Fig 2: The Catalog button will take you to a dedicated section of the App Store to browse and download free course materials*

*Fig 3: Your downloaded material will be stored on your shelves – tap on a cover to access each study guide*

Fig 1: To launch iTunes Match, connect your iPad to your computer, launch iTunes 10. Click on your account details and then click on Learn More next to iTunes Match

Fig 2: You will need to pay a subscription fee to use the service that allows you to store up to 25,000 songs in your iCloud

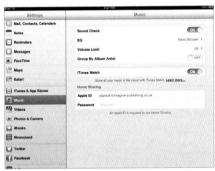

Fig 3: When you subscribe to the service, launch Settings on your iPad, tap on the Music section and then turn iTunes Match on

# "You essentially have access to your entire music collection whenever you want it"

## iTunes Match

As iTunes now works in perfect harmony with Apple's iCloud service, any music that you purchase, regardless of which device you're using to make the purchase, will be automatically pushed to your other iOS 6 devices. iTunes Match is an extension of this service which matches the music on your computer that has been imported from CDs to their digital iTunes Store counterparts, and stores it all in your iCloud so that you have access to your entire music collection whenever you want it. You can find out more in iTunes on your computer (Fig 1).

iTunes determines which songs in your collection are available in the iTunes Store. Any music with a match is automatically added to iCloud for you to listen to any time, on any device. Since there are more than 20 million songs in the iTunes Store, chances are your music is already in iCloud. And for the few songs that aren't, iTunes uploads what it can't match.

Using the service requires a subscription fee of £21.99/$24.99 a year, which you can purchase from iTunes 10 (Fig 2). You must make sure it's activated on iPad by launching Settings and tapping on Music (Fig 3).

# Download media
Instant visual entertainment on your iPad

## 1: Find item
Use the tabs at the bottom of the screen to access the Films and TV Programmes.

## 2: Tap the price
Tap on the price of the item and then tap again when it says Buy.

## 3: Download
The item will be downloaded and will appear in your Videos app.

## 4: Enjoy the show
Tap on your purchase in the Videos app and then sit back and enjoy.

# Download audiobooks

Access a huge range of audiobooks on your iPad

## 1: Tap on Audiobooks

While in the iTunes app, tap Audiobooks down at the bottom.

## 2: Navigate

Use the buttons at the top of the screen to navigate through categories.

## 3: Find a book

Browse what's popular or search for something original and then select it.

## 4: Download and listen

Your audiobook will be added to a section of your Music app.

**Buy or rent**
Some of the films on the iTunes Store can be rented for a short time as well as purchased outright. Tap the option that suits you

**Try before you buy**
If you are unsure of whether to buy or rent a film, you have the option to watch a short preview to help you make up your mind

## Genius

Genius is like your own personal music computer that calculates and sources music based upon what's in your iTunes Library. You may be used to Genius through iTunes 10 on your Mac or PC, but it can be useful through the iTunes iPad app too. To activate Genius, connect your iPad to your computer and then activate the Genius sidebar in iTunes (Fig 1). You'll be able to see the service in effect by clicking on a song in your iTunes Library. Genius can also create playlists and recommend further listening based on what you have previously bought through iTunes.

The way in which Genius works on your iPad is that you can get Genius recommendations through the iTunes app and playlists through the Music app. While in the iTunes app, tap the Genius tab at the top and see all of the recommendations (Fig 2). You can vote on whether you agree with the recommendation to streamline the service next time. You can create Genius playlists in the Music app by tapping on the Genius icon to the right of the playback controls bar at the top of the window. Genius is really a cool feature that's aptly named as it does all your work, keeping your preferences in mind.

Fig 1: Activate Genius through iTunes on your computer; connect your iPad to activate its features in the iTunes and Music apps

Fig 2: Tap the Genius tab at the bottom of the Store to see recommendations

Fig 1: Tap on the Purchased section in the iTunes app to view all of your past buys through the iTunes service

# "Buy a song from iTunes on your iPad, and find it waiting for you on your iPhone"

## iTunes in the Cloud

With iCloud, the music that you purchase in iTunes can appear automatically on all of your iOS 6 devices. You can also download your past iTunes purchases where you want, when you want. iCloud can automatically download new music purchases to all your devices over Wi-Fi – or over a cellular network if you choose. Which means you can buy a song from iTunes on your iPad at home, and find it waiting for you on your iPhone during your morning commute, all without even having to sync between devices.

Any music you have purchased in the past will also be easily accessible. Simply tap on the Purchased section at the bottom of the iTunes app interface (see Fig 1) and you will be able to view an alphabetical list of all of your past purchases. If one of the items isn't currently on your iPad, then highlight it and then tap on the iCloud icon next to the song name (Fig 2). The song will instantly start downloading to your device and will be playable through the Music app. You can also subscribe to iTunes Match, which, as we have previously explored, will match songs in the iTunes catalogue with those ripped from CDs on your computer and allow you to access them anytime you want. You can activate this feature through the Music section in Settings (Fig 3).

Fig 2: Highlight a song not currently on your iPad and then tap the iCloud icon to download it

Fig 3: You can activate the iTunes Match service in the Music section of the Settings app

## Manage downloads
### View what is currently downloading to your device

### 1: Start downloading
Start downloading items and then tap on Downloads at the bottom.

### 2: View downloads
All of the items currently downloading can be viewed in this section.

### 3: Pause download
Tap the pause button next to an item to suspend the download.

### 4: Resume
Tap the arrow icon next to an item to resume downloading and clear the page.

# Pre-order an album
## Stay up-to-date with new releases by pre-ordering

### 1: Find an album
Scroll down and you'll see a Pre-Orders section in the Music Store.

### 2: Tap price
Tap on the the album and note the release date.

### 3: Pre-order album
The price will change to Pre-order Album. Tap on this option.

### 4: Confirm purchase
A message of confirmation will appear. Tap on Pre-order.

## Intelligent search

With so many products readily available on the iTunes Store, thankfully finding them isn't a problem thanks to the intelligent search function that instantly matches the words that you input into the search field with all relevant songs, artists, albums and suchlike. As soon as you start inputting text, the search engine will jump into action by providing a list of possible matches (Fig 1) that will gradually filter down as you write more to the specific item in question – or multiple matches if several products share the same name (which is especially frequent in song titles).

As soon as you see the correct match in the menu of suggestions, you can tap on it in the list to instantly jump to that product. Alternatively, just continue to type in the full title and the list of suggested possibilities will be reduced until only perfect matches are displayed. At this point you can either tap on a suggestion in the list or hit the Search button on the keyboard to initiate the search. When the app directs you to the search results page, you will find the product that you are looking for in the various sections, which include Albums, Songs, iTunes Essentials, Music Videos, Podcasts, Ringtones, books and more (Fig 2).

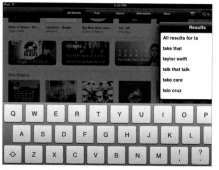

Fig 1: Start typing words into the search field to initiate the rapid response search engine employed by the iTunes Store

Fig 2: The incredibly detailed search results may mean you find albums and artists you weren't aware of

## Not On This iPad
Tap on the tab at the top of the window to see a list of purchased songs not currently on your iPad

## iTunes in the Cloud
Tap on the iCloud icon to download past purchases to your iPad

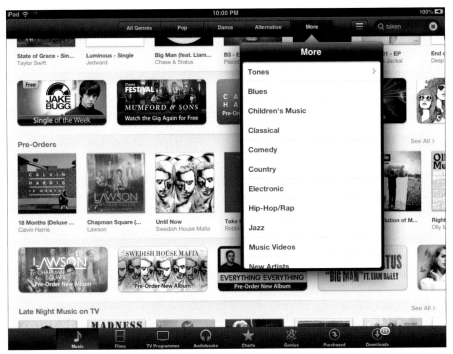

Fig 1: Tap More at the top of the Music section and then choose Tones to be taken to the Tones Store

# "You'll instantly be bombarded with sonic inspiration to spruce up your device"

## The Tones Store

With iOS 6, iTunes now includes the Tones Store, which provides access to a variety of different ringtones and sound effects. Much like any other dedicated section of the iTunes Store – like Music, Films, etc - the Tones Store comes with its own Featured section, Top Charts and various categories, such as Ringtones and Alert Tones. When searching for specific items using the smart search engine, the chances are that the app will throw up ringtones as suggestions, in which case you can jump straight to that product from the search page or visit the Store itself and trawl its wares for effects to purchase and download.

To access the Tones Store on iPad, tap on the Music tab and then hit the More button at the top of the screen (see Fig 1). Tap on the Tones option and you'll be whisked off straight to the Tones Store where you'll instantly be bombarded with sonic inspiration to spruce up your device. Purchasing tones is easy and uses exactly the same process as if you were buying music or film (Fig 2). Simply tap on a price next to a product to make the purchase and download the product. Obviously you can't assign ringtones to your iPad, but you can buy alert tones, which you can assign by launching Settings and choosing Sounds (Fig 3). It always helps to have something different.

Fig 2: The Tones Store is laid out exactly like the other specialist sections of the iTunes Store

Fig 3: Any alert tones you buy can be assigned in the Sounds section in General Settings

# Add an artist alert

Get notified when new material is released

## 1: Connect iPad

Connect your iPad to your Mac or PC and launch iTunes 10 on your computer.

## 2: Tap Home

Tap the Home icon at the top of the iTunes Store interface.

## 3: Access alerts

From the Quick Links menu to the right, click on Alerts.

## 4: Manage alerts

You can now request notification from your favourite bands releasing material.

# Music

Explore the new features of Apple's new-look iPad app and learn how you can play your music with confidence and create epic playlists for any occasion

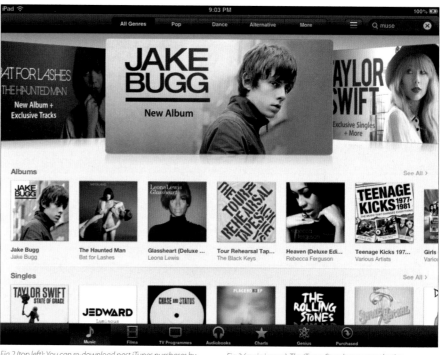

*Fig 1 (above): All music content is accessed through the Music app, which has been recently redesigned*

*Fig 2 (top left): You can re-download past iTunes purchases by tapping on the 'Purchased' section and pressing the cloud icon*

*Fig 3 (main image): The iTunes Store has a vast selection of tracks to download for your Music app*

## Use it to:

- **Play music**
  First and foremost, the Music app is an MP3 player.

- **Purchase content**
  Visit the iTunes Store in a single tap to buy new music.

- **Organise your albums**
  Your music is neatly arranged, making it easy to find.

- **Make playlists**
  Compile your essential mixes within minutes.

- **Get recommendations**
  Let Genius create perfect playlists based on the track currently playing.

- **Control the EQ**
  You have total control over how your music sounds.

# Listen to your tunes

## Learn how to get the most out of your Music app

### Import songs and podcasts

Formerly known as the iPod app, Music is an iOS 6 amalgamation of new features and ideas that makes for an intuitive music player. But to get the most out of it you will naturally need music to play through it. There are various ways to get music onto your iPad. You can go the old-fashioned method of connecting your iPad up to your computer and then manually transferring songs from your iTunes library, or you can purchase new material on your iPad using the iTunes app (Fig 3). From here you can get songs, entire albums and audiobooks; just purchase through iTunes and they will be

downloaded and placed within your Music app, ready to play (Fig 1).

You can also utilise the power of iCloud to instantly get songs that you have downloaded in the past (Fig 2), by tapping on the 'Purchased' section in the iTunes app, selecting content that is 'Not On This iPad' (from the tab at the top), highlighting a song and then tapping the cloud icon next to it. You can also subscribe to iTunes Match (£21.99/$24.99 a year), which notes down all of the music on your computer and then matches it up to that on the iTunes Store to ensure you have full access to your music collection at all times.

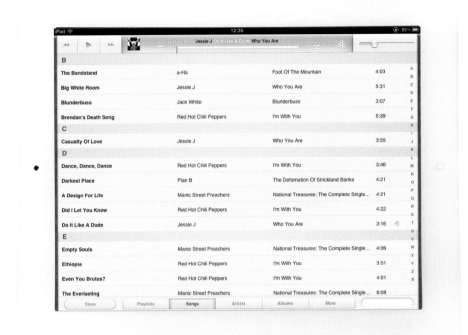

*Fig 1: Tap the Genius atom icon to the right of the playback controls to set your personal Genius to work*

# "Genius finds other songs that go great with the one currently playing"

## Genius

When you're listening to a song you really love, Music's Genius feature finds other songs that go great with it and creates a playlist that you'll love even more. Once Genius has created your perfect playlist, you can play it, save it or give it another go.

While playing tunes through the Music app, tap on the Genius icon that is to the right of the playback controls (it resembles an atom diagram) and Genius will note down your current song and find other songs that sit comfortably next to it in your library to create a playlist (Fig 1). Tap on the 'Playlists' tab at the

bottom of the screen to access your playlists and tap on the one called 'Genius Playlist' to see what it came up with (Fig 2).

You can play this list, refresh it to mix it up a bit and tap the 'Save' button to ensure that it is safely stored on your device for future use (Fig 3). By trawling your library and creating playlists, Genius can come up with sound scores to accompany any gathering, situation or mood – such as parties or car journeys – and you'll hear mixes that you probably wouldn't have thought of yourself and get the opportunity to reappreciate songs that you may have forgotten you even had.

*Fig 2: Genius will come up with original playlists to suit any occasion. Go to the 'Playlists' section to see what it comes up with*

*Fig 3: You can listen to the new playlists, refresh them to mix things up or save for them future use*

## Rate albums

### Provide some feedback on records that matter to you

### 1: Tap Store

While in the Music app, hit the 'Store' button in the bottom-left corner.

### 2: Find an album

Tap on a song or album to bring up the floating info page.

### 3: Tap Ratings and Reviews

Tap Ratings and Reviews to see what others think of the album

### 4: Rate it

Tap the stars to rate the material and then tap on the background.

# Music

## Playback controls

You can play/pause and rewind/fast-forward your tracks using the basic control buttons and scrub through it by dragging your finger along the scrubbing bar at the top

## Store access

Shop for new songs instantly by tapping the 'Store' icon in the bottom-left corner to go straight to the iTunes Store

## Genius

Tap this icon to get Genius working on your behalf to create cracking playlists that relate to the song you are listening to

## Your songs

All of the songs stored in your Music app are arranged into sections for easy access, all of which are accessible from the options at the bottom of the interface

## Manage your playlists

The more music that you start to compile on your iPad, the more album chaff you'll have to sift through in order to get to the good stuff – which is where the Playlists feature of your Music app comes in very handy.

Tap on the 'Playlists' button at the bottom of the Music app interface and then tap on 'New' in the top-right corner of the screen to create a new list (Fig 1). Give your playlist a name and tap to save. You will then be guided to your songs database, whereupon you can start adding tunes to your list. To

select a song, either tap on the title of the song or the '+' button to the right of each song (Fig 2). Once you have added a sufficient amount, tap the 'Done' button. After creating your new playlist, you can now manage it by either tapping the red icon to delete songs or pressing and holding your finger on the list icon to the right of the track and then dragging it up or down to edit the running order of your playlist (Fig 3). Again, when you are happy, tap 'Done' and your playlist will be added to the 'Playlists' section for easy access when you need it later.

*Fig 1: Tap 'New' in the 'Playlists' section to create, name and save a new playlist*

# "The Playlists feature comes in very handy for listening to your favourite songs and avoiding album chaff"

*Fig 2: Select songs from your library to add to your playlist. Tap the title or the '+' icon to select tracks*

*Fig 3: Press and hold on the list icon to drag and rearrange the running order of your playlist*

Fig 1: Tap on songs to start playing them and then use the playback controls to pause and skip tracks

# "The playback controls in the Music app are simple and easy to use"

## Play your music

Playing music is what your dedicated Music app is all about, and the controls that you are given to perform this task are simple and easy to use. You can play music by accessing your music collection via the 'Playlists', 'Songs', 'Artists' and 'Albums' categories at the bottom of the main Music app interface (Fig 2).

Simply tap on a song to start playing it. The playback controls will become available at the top of the screen. The main window displays the name and artist, the running time and links to Genius and repeat options. A volume

slider to the right lets you quickly adjust the level of sound, while controls to the left allow you to play/pause and skip tracks (Fig 1). You can also use the scrub bar in the main window to move rapidly forwards or backwards through a track. If you want to make fine adjustments to the sound then launch your Settings app and tap on the Music section. Turn on the 'EQ' and you'll be able to adjust the levels to suit the ambience (Fig 3). Finally, don't forget that you can access audiobooks through the Music app by tapping on the 'More' option.

Fig 2: Use the categories at the bottom of the window to find your music easily and create new playlists

Fig 3: Go to the Music section in Settings to activate the EQ option and make adjustments to the sound

## Delete songs
How to erase tracks to make room for more

### 1: Find a song
Trawl through your library until you find a song you want to erase.

### 2: Swipe left
Touch the song and swipe your finger to the left.

### 3: Tap Delete
A 'Delete' button will appear. Tap it to instantly delete the song.

### 4: Use anywhere
Use this technique to delete songs in any category.

# Videos

If you want to turn your iPad into a portable entertainment system then you'll need to know your way around the Videos app

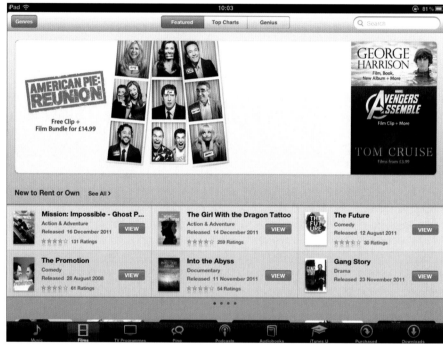

## Use it to:

- **Play videos**
  Watch movies from the iTunes Store and your computer (via Wi-Fi).

- **Take full control**
  Skip to the best bits using high-speed scrubbing.

- **Buy or rent**
  The iTunes Store features a great selection of videos.

- **Share at home**
  Get your films beamed wirelessly to your Apple TV.

- **Watch in hi-res**
  Watch films in 1080p on the new iPad.

- **Manage the catalogue**
  Each video is categorised within the app.

*Fig 1 (top left): Tap on a video to bring up its info page and then tap Play to start watching it*

*Fig 2 (main image): A great selection of films, shows and music videos awaits you at the Store*

*Fig 3 (bottom left): Touch the screen while a video is playing to access the playback controls*

# Watch great videos

Transform your iPad into your own portable multiplex with the Videos app

### Play videos

Your iPad is ideal for watching movies and TV shows. The large HD screen makes it a very versatile device for enjoying visual entertainment around the house.

To start watching videos on your iPad you must first get some content – by connecting your iPad to iTunes and transferring MP4 video files, or by purchasing content from the iTunes Store direct from your iPad. There is a wide range of visual entertainment on offer in the Store (Fig 2), including great films and TV shows that you can browse by tapping on their respective section button at the bottom

of the iTunes app interface. You can also purchase music videos from the Music section.

To watch your videos, launch the Videos app and, depending on what you have on your device, you will be able to access your content by tapping a button at the top that represents the Movies, Music Videos and TV Shows sections. When a video is displayed, tap on it to bring up an information page (Fig 1) and then tap the play button to start watching. The video will play full screen and you can touch the screen to bring up the playback controls, including play/pause, high-speed scrubbing and volume controls (Fig 3).

Fig 1: You can switch between Movies and TV shows using the tabs at the top of the screen

# "You can browse your iTunes videos without downloading them to your iPad"

## Home Sharing

If, like us, you have ever wanted to use your iPad to watch a video that you have on iTunes on your desktop computer, then Home Sharing is for you. Your iPad can wirelessly connect to your computer's iTunes, so you can browse your iTunes library's videos without downloading them to your iPad. You can share television shows and movies that you've purchased, but not movies that you've rented.

To turn on Home Sharing you must first activate it on your computer by opening iTunes, going to 'Advanced' on the top toolbar and selecting 'Turn On Home Sharing' (Fig 2). You'll need to enter your Apple ID and password. Now, on your iPad, go to the Settings app and the Video tab, then enable Home Sharing here by entering your Apple ID again (Fig 3).

Now open up the Videos app and you should see a 'Shared' tab towards the top-right of the screen. Tap this, and you will see the videos on your computer's hard drive (Fig 1). Tap the one you wish to view on your tablet and enjoy. Now you can watch videos from your computer – even if someone else is using it!

Fig 2: Make sure you activate Home Sharing on iTunes on your computer by going to Advanced>Turn On Home Sharing

Fig 3: Go to the Settings app and then Video; add your Apple ID to enable Sharing on iPad

## Video scrub speeds
Choose how quickly you can scrub through your videos

### 1: Watch a video
Start watching a video through your Videos app and then touch the screen.

### 2: Playback controls
This reveals the scrub bar (top), play/pause options and volume level (below).

### 3: Move slider
Scrub through videos by moving your finger along the bar at the top.

### 4: Jump
You can also jump to any point on a video by simply tapping it.

# Videos

**Scrubbing bar**
Slide your finger along this bar to fast-forward the video or rewind. Slide your finger down the screen to adjust the speed

**Screen size**
Tap this button to make the current video fill the entire screen or revert the video back to its original format

**Playback controls**
Touch the screen while a video is playing to display the controls. These include play/ pause and high-speed scrubbing

**Done**
The 'Done' button will exit the current video. You can determine if it picks up where you left off next time by going to the Videos section in Settings

**Volume controls**
Increase or decrease the volume of the video by sliding your finger along this section

## AirPlay with videos

If you're lucky enough to own an Apple TV, then you can stream videos from your iPad directly to the television using AirPlay. The best feature of this service is there there are no wires necessary. Like the previous occasions where we have used AirPlay, you need to make sure your Apple TV and iPad are connected to the same Wi-Fi network.

You can check which network you are on by clicking on Wi-Fi in the Settings app.

Now open the video that you're looking to stream to the television. When it's playing, tap the AirPlay icon (a hollow rectangle with a solid triangle) that's now found on the regular playback control bar. A menu should pop up with 'iPad' ticked (Fig 2). Tap 'Apple TV' to start streaming your video to the television within

a couple of seconds. It is worth noting that you cannot have the same video playing on both your iPad and the Apple TV – so it'll have to be either your iPad or your Apple TV. While the video is streaming on Apple TV, the iPad will merely carry a blank screen (Fig 3). To quit streaming, hit the blue 'Done' button to the top left of the iPad, which will take you back to your videos.

*Fig 1: Both devices must be connected to the same network*

*Fig 2: The device you're playing the video on will be ticked*

*Fig 3: You're unable to play the video on both Apple TV and iPad*

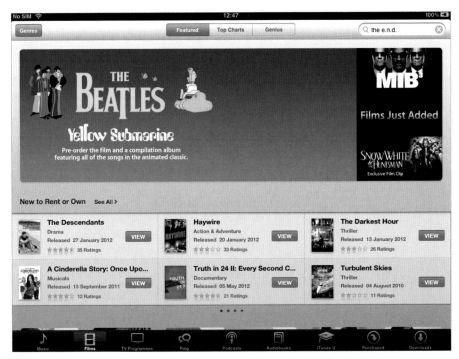

Fig 1: Browse the Films and TV Programmes sections of the iTunes Store, via the iTunes app, to find plenty of inspiration

# "In the iTunes Store, you can buy the video outright or rent it for a period of time"

## Rent and buy videos

As we have already mentioned, the best, most convenient source of video content for your iPad is through the iTunes Store, which is instantly accessible via your iTunes app. Launch the latter and then tap on the Films or TV Programmes buttons ('Movies' and 'TV Shows' if using a US Store account) at the bottom of the screen to start exploring the wide range of content available (Fig 1).

While browsing the store for videos, when you see one you're interested in, tap the 'View' button next to the title to bring up a floating info screen that includes plot summary, credits, details and your purchase options (Fig 2). You'll see what videos are selectable in HD and SD resolutions, ratings and related content. You can buy the video outright or rent it for a period of time. With this option you pay to download the video to your device. You then have 30 days to watch the film, but only 48 hours from the moment you press play to finish watching it. You can also watch a short trailer from the information page (Fig 3) and tell a friend about your selection. If you decide not to purchase the video at this stage, simply tap the background, which will take you to the previous section.

Fig 2: Tap 'View' to discover more about each video and also get the prices for buying it or renting it

Fig 3: You can watch short trailers from the floating info screen, which will play through the Videos app interface

## Delete videos
### How to remove what you no longer need

### 1: Choose category
Pick a category of videos from the options available at the top.

### 2: Tap Edit
Now tap the 'Edit' button in the top-right corner of the screen.

### 3: Tap cross
Tap the cross that appears next to the video you want to delete.

### 4: Confirm process
Finally, confirm that you wish to delete and it shall be done.

# Safari

The Safari app is your window to the worldwide web. We give you our guide
to this brilliant web-browsing app which puts the internet at your fingertips

## Use it to:

- **Browse the web**
  Trawl your favourite sites on your iPad.

- **Sync your tabs**
  Keep your tabs in sync, thanks to iCloud.

- **Use Safari Reader**
  Read top stories in a clean, uncluttered window.

- **Save your stories**
  Use Reading List to read offline later.

- **Keep bookmarks**
  Access your favourite sites with a single press.

- **Go super-size**
  Master full-screen viewing.

- **Share websites**
  Post your favourite sites to Facebook and Twitter.

Fig 1 (below top): Pinch and expand your fingers to zoom in on pages and swipe to scroll

Fig 2 (below bottom): The share icon provides many options, including bookmarking all your favourite websites

Fig 3 (main image): By adding a bookmark to the Home screen, you can tap it to launch in Safari

# Browse the web

## Safari is not only a very good browser, but one of the simplest to use in terms of functionality and navigation

### Surfing with ease

Browsing the internet on your iPad is a pleasurable experience made easy by the touchscreen interface that your tablet device employs and simple gestures that mean you can touch links to go to the respective page, pinch and expand your fingers to zoom in and out, and swipe your finger up or down the screen to scroll the pages (Fig 1).

A simple interface also makes it easy to bookmark your favourite pages. To the left of the address bar is the sharing icon that you can touch to bring up a list of Safari options (Fig 2). We'll come to some of these options later but the Bookmark option, provides all the functionality you need to store your favourite pages for easy access. Here you can rename the bookmark, so rather than store it as the long (and often convoluted) web address, you can shorten it to something snappier. Tap on the Bookmarks option and you'll be able to store it in the Bookmarks Menu – accessible from this menu – or save in the Bookmarks Bar, which sits along the top of the page under the address bar and provides quick and easy access to your favourite sites. From the share menu you can also choose the Add to Home Screen option. This will fashion the bookmark into an app-style icon that you can tap on from your Home screen to launch Safari and the page simultaneously, saving you loads more time (Fig 3).

*Fig 1: You can open new tabs by tapping the '+' icon to the right of the tabs list*

# "Research is easy through Safari as you can keep your most important sites open"

## iCloud tabs

iCloud tabs is a new feature of iOS 6 that allows Safari users to sync their tabs across multiple devices that are all running the same iCloud account. iCloud tabs are easily accessed by tapping the iCloud icon to the left of the address bar - this brings up the iCloud tabs menu, showing all of the tabs that are open on every device linked by an iCloud account. This makes research easy through Safari as you can keep your most important sites open and not have to worry about which device you've originally opened them on.

Adding new tabs is easy. While on any webpage, simply press the '+' icon to the far-right of the tabs to open a new window (Fig 1) and instantly store the page you were on previously as a tab. In iOS 6, you can open as many tabs as you like (although it does get a little awkward with ten or more) and you can close tabbed webpages by tapping on the small 'X' icon situated to the left of each tab (Fig 3). To enable iCloud tabs, you'll need to be signed into your iCloud account and have the option enabled under the Settings app on each device you want to use.

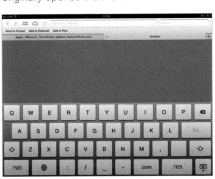

*Fig 2: When a new tab is opened Safari will automatically focus on the adress bar so you can navigate to a new site*

*Fig 3: You can close any of your nine available tabs by pressing the 'X' icon to the left of the tab name*

## Set up iCloud Tabs
### Access your tabs from any Mac, iPhone or iPad

### 1: Enable iCloud
Under the iCloud section of the Settings App, log in with your account details.

### 2: Tap the toggle
Ensure that Safari's toggle is set to On under iCloud in the Settings app.

### 3: In the cloud
Open up Safari and tap on the iCloud icon next to the address bar.

### 4: Tap 'n' Load
To load a tab from one of your other devices, simply tap on its title.

# Safari

## Share it all
Tapping this icon will bring up a number of options to share the page you're on, as well as options to print it

## Tabbed pages
You can keep webpages open simultaneously by opening them as separate tabs and even sync them across all of your devices using your iCloud account

## Address bar
If you know a website address then type it directly in here. If the page is available for Safari Reader, then the Reader icon will appear in the bar

## Search engine
By default, the Google search engine is built into Safari, but you can easily change this in Settings

> "Safari Reader is a great feature that enables web articles to be displayed without ads or clutter"

## Safari Reader

As we have already explored, reading webpages in Safari is made easy through the intuitive interface, but one of Safari's stand-out features - Safari Reader - makes things even easier. Safari Reader enables web articles to be displayed without ads or clutter, so you can read away without distractions.

Not all webpages support this feature, but those that do are instantly apparent because a small Reader icon will be displayed in the address bar at the top of the window (Fig 1). When you see this icon, tap on it to activate the Safari Reader feature and a new window

will be opened that strips away all of the ads, links and unnecessary clutter to leave pure, simple text that can be read and digested easily (Fig 2). You can also change the font through Safari Reader to make it even bigger and easier to read (Fig 3). To do this, tap the font icon in the top-left corner of the Safari Reader page and choose between the default or enhanced font.

When you have finished reading an article through Safari Reader, simply tap on the Reader icon again (this time it will be displayed in purple) to return to the original page and continue your browsing.

*Fig 1: Webpages that support the Safari Reader feature are indicated by a small Reader icon in the address bar*

*Fig 2: By tapping the icon, all of the clutter is stripped away from the page, making it much easier to read*

*Fig 3: You can also increase the font size to make the pages even easier to read*

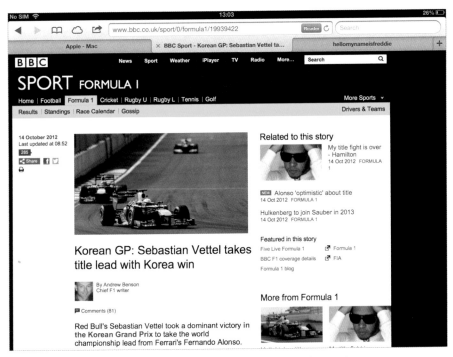

*Fig 1: Add articles to your Reading List by tapping the arrow icon and selecting the Add to Reading List option*

*Fig 2: Access your articles by tapping the book icon and then choosing the Reading List section*

*Fig 3: To ensure that your Reading List articles are synced across devices, go to Settings>iCloud and ensure Safari is activated*

# "All of the pages saved to your Reading List will be synced across all your iOS devices"

## Offline Reading List

iOS 5 brought Reading List to Safari. This feature enables you to save interesting articles to read later. With iOS 6, reading lists went offline, meaning you don't need an internet connection to view your saved content. What's more, thanks to iCloud, all of the pages saved to your Reading List will be synced across all of your iOS devices. This means that you can now save a page to your Reading List on your iPhone and then read pick up from where you left off on your iPad later (see Fig 3) at your own convenience.

To save an article to your Reading List, tap the Share button to the left of the address bar in the main Safari window while the page you wish to save is displayed in the main window. Select the 'Add to Reading List' option (Fig 1). To then access the articles saved to your Reading List, tap the book icon at the top of the window. Tap the Reading List section at the bottom of your bookmarks list (Fig 2), and all of the articles that you have saved to your Reading List will be present. From here, you can filter articles to show those you haven't read using the controls at the top of the list.

# Clear your history
## Here's how to cover your internet tracks

## 1: Go to Bookmarks
While in Safari, tap the book icon and then go to the History section.

## 2: Clear History
All of your recent history is displayed. Tap the Clear History button to erase it.

## 3: Go to Settings
Launch your Settings app and then tap on the Safari section from the list.

## 4: Clear Cookies
Here you will see an option called Clear Cookies and Data. Tap this.

# Private Browsing
## Keep the sites you visit private

### 1: Why go private?
Activate Private Browsing to prevent others from seeing your web history.

### 2: Go to Settings
Quit Safari and, from your Home screen, launch your Settings app.

### 3: Tap Safari
Select the Safari section from the list on the left of the screen.

### 4: Go private
Under Privacy, turn the Private Browsing slider to the On position.

## Your Bookmarks
The pages you bookmark can either be added to the Bookmarks Bar (at the top of the window) or to your Bookmarks Menu

## Reading List
All articles that you decide to save to your Reading List to read offline later will be added to this list

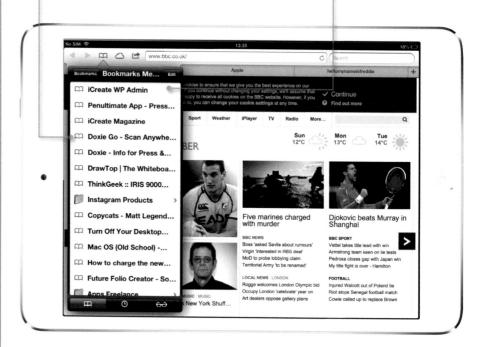

## Bookmarks Bar
As we have explored, there are numerous ways to save and store your favourite webpages to keep them close at hand and one of the best ways is to save them to your Bookmarks Bar. This is essentially a spread of bookmarked sites that run across the top of your Safari web browser, underneath the address bar. From here, you can access far quicker than scrolling through your Bookmarks Menu. To add a new bookmark to your Bookmarks bar, tap the share icon to the left of the address bar and then choose the Bookmark option (Fig 1).

You can then trim the name of the bookmark or rename it to something short and sweet, and then choose a destination to save it to (Fig 2). Tap the Bookmarks section and then select Bookmarks Bar. When you're happy to add the site, tap Save and the name of the site will appear at the top of your Safari window for easy access. You can edit the sites on your Bookmarks Bar by tapping the book icon followed by Bookmarks Bar and then tapping the Edit button in the top-right corner to rename, re-order or delete sites.

What's more, your bookmarks bar will sync across every device via your iCloud account.

*Fig 1: Start adding sites to your Bookmarks Bar by tapping on the arrow icon and choosing Add Bookmark*

*Fig 2: Trim the titles, choose the destination and then hit Save to save sites to your Bookmarks Bar*

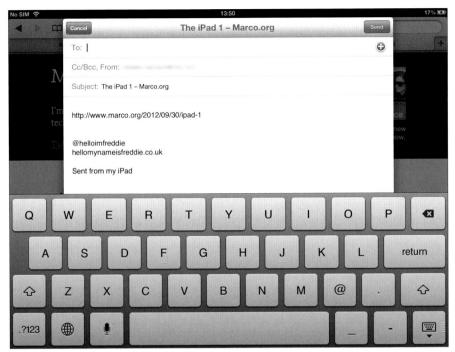

Fig 1: Choosing the Mail Link to this Page option allows you to send an email from within Safari

# "You can tweet from a range of default Apple apps - Safari included"

## Sharing websites

Sometimes you may see something on the web that amazes or outrages you to the extent that you simply have to share it with others. Thankfully, Safari is very accommodating in this department and provides a few options to quickly share your online discoveries with others.

These options are all accessible through the share icon, situated to the left of the address bar which, as we have already discovered, is your gateway to a host of Safari features. From this menu you can select the Mail Link to this Page option - Tweet, Facebook, Message or Print (Fig 3). The first option enables you to

send an email of the page link directly out from Safari without having to copy and paste anything into Mail (Fig 1). You'll be able to add a message in the composer window, which also contains a link to the site that the recipients can click or tap on. The subject is also the site's title.

Selecting the Message option will copy the link into a new message composer so you can send it to any of your iMessage contacts.

Tapping either Facebook or Tweet will bring up a Share Sheet (Fig 2) that allows you to Tweet or post the link as a Facebook status without leaving Safari. You'll need to set up Facebook and Twitter in Settings first, though.

Fig 2: As Twitter is integrated into iOS 6, you can tweet straight from a host of Apple apps

Fig 3: Provided you have an AirPrint printer, you can also print pages out from the Safari app

## Find a phrase
### How to quickly search for words and phrases

### 1: Tap search field
While on a webpage, tap the Google search field in the top-right corner.

### 2: Type words
Just above the keyboard is a Find on Page option. Start typing into this.

### 3: Find on page
All words and phrases that correspond will be zoomed in on and highlighted.

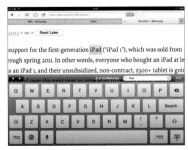

### 4: Cycle options
Use the arrows next to the text window to skip to the next or previous match.

# Mail

Learn how to compose and send emails, organise accounts and get all of your emails from all of your accounts streamed to the same inbox

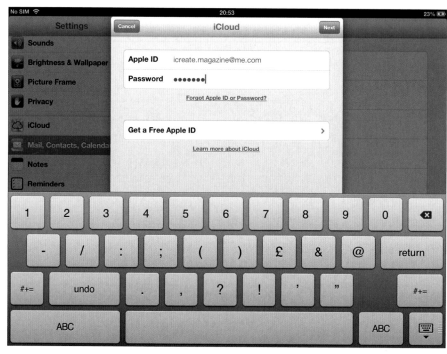

## Use it to:

- **Link to an account**
  You can activate the Mail app with any valid email address and password.

- **Send and receive**
  Keep up to date with incoming mails and quickly send out messages.

- **Manage accounts**
  Add multiple personal and professionals accounts.

- **Organise messages**
  Store and save messages safely away.

- **Format your mail**
  Tweak the text in your emails for more impact.

- **Arrange the interface**
  Drag and arrange names as you compose emails.

*Fig 1 (top left):
Set up the push
frequency in
'Mail, Contacts,
Calendars'
in Settings*

*Fig 2 (bottom
left): Tap the pen
icon to compose
an email. Just fill
in all the info and
hit 'Send'*

*Fig 3 (main
image): Enter
an address and
password to add
an account to the
iPad Mail app*

# Managing your email with Mail
### Easy to set up and use, Mail is designed to make your life easier

## Send and receive emails

If you are using the Mail app for the first time, you will need to set up and link an account to the app. This is a quick and easy process that requires no more than a valid and active email address and an account password (see Fig 3). Once set up, select your account in the 'Inboxes' section of the Mailboxes column and all new messages will instantly be downloaded for that account.

You can determine when all new emails are pushed from the servers to your mailbox by launching your Settings app and tapping on the 'Mail, Contacts, Calendars' section and then selecting the 'Fetch New Data' option.

Activate the Push function to ensure that you get all new mail as soon as possible. You should tick the 'Every 15 Minutes' option to get any new mail as soon as possible in the event that Push fails (Fig 1). Your device will now automatically scan for new mail every time you launch the app.

To send an email, simply tap on the page icon in the top-right corner of the interface and a blank email will appear. Fill in the recipient's address (and any CCs or BCCs you'd like), enter a subject and some body text and then hit 'Send' (Fig 2). You can also mail out attachments, such as photos, from within the app with a few quick taps - all thanks to iOS 6.

## Access all emails from all accounts in one inbox

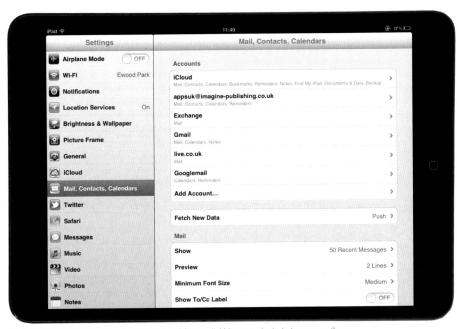

Fig 1: Go to 'Mail, Contacts, Calendars' in Settings and then tap 'Add Account…' to include a new mailbox

### 1: Set up multiple accounts

Go to 'Mail, Contacts, Calendars' in Settings and 'Add Account…'

# "Mail is versatile enough to incorporate virtually any type of email account"

## Manage multiple accounts

It's very rare these days that people just have one email address. At the very least most would have a work and a personal account. The Mail app is versatile enough to incorporate virtually any type of email account with a few easy steps and, handily, you can stream all of your mail from all of your accounts into one main inbox. This makes it easy to track all aspects of your life simultaneously.

To add a new account, launch your Settings app and then go to the 'Mail, Contacts, Calendars' section. Under the 'Accounts' section at the top of the page, you'll see the option to 'Add Account…' (Fig 1); tap this

and then choose the type of account you will be adding. These include Gmail, Yahoo!, AOL, Hotmail and more (Fig 2). Once you have selected the account, enter a name, email address and password for that account and, after a few seconds of verification, the account will be added to your active inboxes within the Mail app. Launch Mail and tap on an inbox in the Mailboxes column to view only the messages applicable to that account. Any emails you send from here will also be assigned to your specific email address for that account. While in the Mailboxes column, you can also tap 'All Inboxes' to get all mail directed into one handy inbox (Fig 3).

### 2: Add accounts

Select the type of account to add and enter the email address and password.

### 3: Open Mail

Launch your Mail app and then tap on the 'All Inboxes' option.

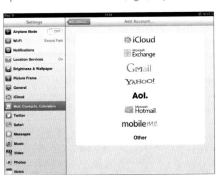

Fig 2: You will need to choose the type of account you are adding. If you don't see the applicable option initially, just tap 'Other'

Fig 3: Tap on an individual inbox in the Mailboxes column or tap 'All Inboxes' to see all of your emails in one place

### 4: Get all mail

All of your mail from all of your accounts will be displayed here.

## Your inboxes
You can access each mailbox from your different accounts by tapping on them in the 'Mailboxes' column

## All Inboxes
If you have multiple accounts then tap on 'All Inboxes' to view all of your emails from all of your accounts in one place

## Composing emails
Tap on this icon in the top-right corner of the interface to start composing a new email. Your address will show up in accordance with the account you are using

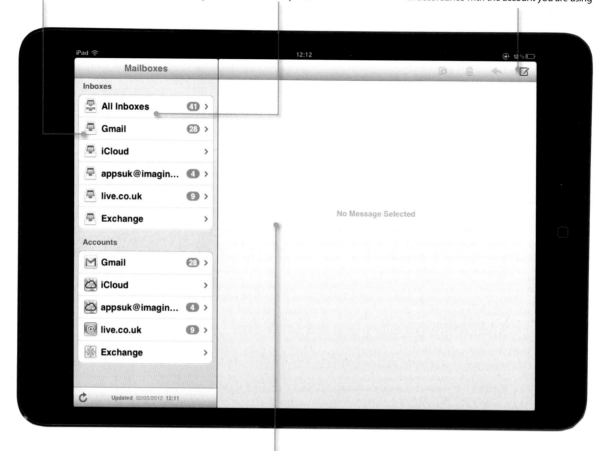

## Your emails
When you tap on an email in your inbox it will be displayed in the main window, whereupon you can file, delete or reply to the email

## Customise emails
When crafting emails, you may want to make them more engaging for others to read by formatting the text. Tucked away within the Mail app are all kinds of tools to help you get your emails looking good.

To format an email, you simply need to press and hold on a word until the magnifying glass appears. Release your finger and then a floating menu appears that lets you select the word you have focused on or select all of the text in the email (see Fig 1). When the required text has been highlighted, a new floating bar will appear that provides instant editing options including 'Cut' and 'Paste'. If you tap the arrow here, options to bold up or italicise the text and change the Quote Level will be revealed. Tap the first option for Bold, Italics and Underline text options. The option to add

photos or videos to your email is also available here and takes just a few quick taps.

You can also personalise your outgoing emails by adding a signature. The default one, 'Sent from my iPad', can be changed

within Settings. Tap on 'Mail, Contacts, Calendars' and then scroll down to the 'Signature' option before changing the text that appears at the end of your emails to something less pretentious (Fig 2).

*Fig 1: Highlight text in your emails and then use the floating toolbar to reveal the formatting options available*

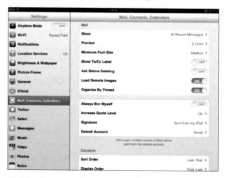

*Fig 2: To change your signature, launch Settings and then tap on the 'Mail, Contacts, Calendars' section*

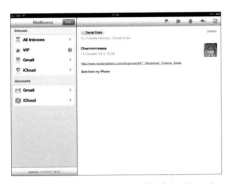

*Fig 2: The VIP Mailbox you've set up should feel far less cluttered than your main, unified inbox*

*Fig 3: VIPs get their own Notification Center options in the settings app to keep you contstantly updated*

# "This feature really works well when you add a small group of people"

## Set up VIP mailboxes

The new features introduced into Mail with iOS 6 are, for the most part, subtle, but there's one that stands out from the crowd. That feature is VIP Mailboxes.

VIP Mailboxes allows you to tackle email overload and see emails from only the most important contacts in your burgeoning address book. To make the most of this feature, you'll first need to select some VIPS. To do this, find a message from someone you'd like to add to your VIP list, tap on their name in the From field and then, in the pop-up

that appears, tap Add to VIP (Fig 1). Once this is done, you'll find a new inbox listed in the Mailboxes sidebar called VIP (Fig 2). Tapping on that will only show messages from people you've added to your VIPs list.

You can add as many VIPs to Mail as you'd like, but this feature really works well when you only add a small group of people such as family or the team you work with.

What's more, you can adjust your Notifications in the Settings App so that Mail only notifies you when you receive emails from your VIPS (Fig 3).

*Fig 1: You can add anyone who has sent you an email to your VIPs list for VIP Mailboxes*

## Mark/flag messages

Organise your messages with just a few simple taps

### 1: Go to inbox
While in a mailbox, highlight a message in the list to the left.

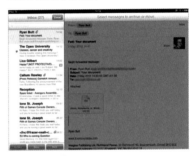

### 2: Tap Edit
Tap the 'Edit' button in the top-left corner of the column.

### 3: Tap to tick
Place a tick next to the message and then tap 'Mark'.

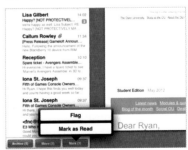

### 4: Choose option
You can now choose to 'Flag' the message or 'Mark as Read'.

## Searching Mail

### With iOS 6 you get plenty of options to help you search

### 1: Tap Search

While in Mail, tap the search field at the top of the inbox to start your search.

### 2: Enter text

Use the keyboard to enter keywords to search for within your emails.

### 3: Set criteria

Use the 'From', 'To', 'Subject' or 'All' tabs to focus your search.

### 4: Results

Emails that contain matches will be listed and you can cycle through them.

### Edit your inbox

You can tap 'Edit' at the top of your inbox to manage your messages, including marking them as read and flagging them

### Easy archive

To quickly archive mails, highlight the message and swipe your finger across it in the inbox list, then tap the 'Archive' option

## Move and organise messages

If you get mail from all of your accounts streamed into one inbox, it can be tricky to keep track of important emails. So it's useful that you can move messages around and store them safely for times of need.

To store a message in your archive, ensure that the message in question has been highlighted in the inbox to the left of the screen and then swipe your finger across the message (either left to right or vice versa) to reveal an 'Archive' button (Fig 1). Tap this and the highlighted message will be moved to your archive. To access messages from your

archive, go back to the main Mailboxes screen and then tap on the relevant account under the 'Accounts' section. The left-hand column will then display all of your email folders (including Inbox, Drafts and Sent Mail), tap on the box icon to see your archived items. You can also archive emails by tapping the box icon in the top-right corner of the screen.

If you just want to move emails between accounts, highlight an email in your inbox and then tap on the folder (with down arrow) icon in the top-right toolbar. You will now be prompted to select a mailbox to move the highlighted message into (Fig 2).

*Fig 1: Highlight a message in your inbox and then swipe your finger across to reveal the hidden 'Archive' option*

*Fig 2: Simply select a mailbox to move a highlighted email into to complete the task*

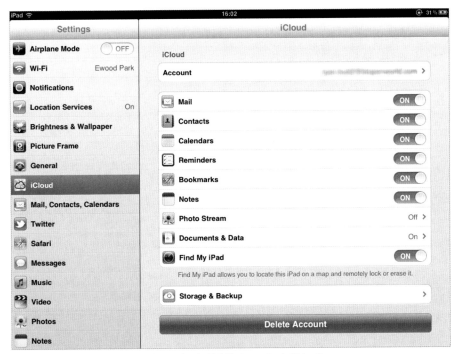

Fig 1: Go to the iCloud section of Settings and ensure that the Mail slider is moved to the 'On' position

# "iCloud automatically pushes new email messages to all your devices"

## Manage your iCloud account

When you set up iCloud, you not only get a free iCloud.com email account, iCloud automatically pushes new email messages to all your devices too. So your inbox is up to date everywhere you check it and all of your folders are kept in sync, no matter which device you're using.

This means that if you read an email on one device then it will be automatically marked as read in the Mail app on your other iOS 6 iCloud-enabled devices. Likewise, if you reply to an email then this will also be reflected on your other devices. To use iCloud with

Mail, launch your Settings app and then tap on the 'iCloud' section in the list to the left. Ensure that the Mail slider is moved to the 'On' position (Fig 1) on all of your iOS 5 devices that are logged into the same iCloud account and everything else will happen seamlessly behind the scenes.

You can check and manage your free me.com account in the Mail app by tapping on Mailboxes (Fig 2) and then selecting the iCloud account listed under the 'Accounts' section at the bottom of the column. Tap on the page icon to start composing an email from within this account (Fig 3).

Fig 2: You can tap on your free iCloud.com account from the main Mailboxes screen

Fig 3: When you now compose an email it will be matched to that account

## Arrange recipients

Organise your intended recipients quickly and easily

### 1: Compose an email

Start composing an email and then tap the blue '+' icon.

### 2: Choose contacts

Choose the intended recipients from your Contacts list.

### 3: Hold a name

Press and hold on a name to move it to a different field.

### 4: Move to field

Drag the name down and you'll be able to place it in 'Cc' or 'Bcc'.

# Calendar

How the iPad's intuitive personal organiser app can be used to ensure that
your working, social and home lives run as smoothly as possible

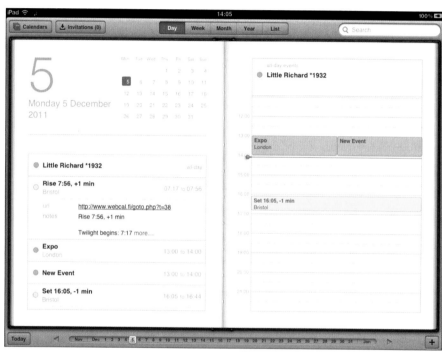

## Use it to:

- **Schedule events**
  Schedule new appointments with a single tap.

- **Change views**
  View the previous/next days, weeks, months or years.

- **Sync important dates**
  Birthdays and key dates from Contacts are instantly synced in the Calendar.

- **Work with iCloud**
  Sync your calendars across all Apple devices.

- **Keep multiple calendars**
  Manage multiple calendars running simultaneously.

- **Invite contacts**
  Send out invites to key events direct from the app.

**Tuesday**
**9**

*Fig 1 (top left): You can change the view by pressing the tabs at the top*

*Fig 2 (main image): The default 'Day' view presents all of the info regarding the current day that you could ever wish for*

*Fig 3 (bottom left): Create new events by tapping the page or '+' icon in the lower right corner*

# Make a date with Calendar
### The iPad Calendar app will ensure that your life is easier to manage

## The Calendar interface

When you launch your Calendar app you will be presented with a wall of information to help you organise your day – and every other day, for that matter. On the default 'Day' view (see Fig 2), you'll get the day's date bigged up in the top-left corner along with the complete calendar month. Any applicable events will be presented at the bottom of the same page and the opposite page will be the day broken down into half-hour segments. You then press and hold on a line to add a new event, entering the various start and end times and inviting people from your Contacts to attend.

A slider at the bottom of the interface allows you to quickly scrub through the current calendar month and you can also change the view with the tabs at the top of the screen. Using these you can view your calendar by Week, Month, Year (Fig 1) or List. You can also search for specific events by entering keywords into the search field and activate all of your synced calendars using the 'Calendars' button in the top-left corner. Finally, if you yourself have received an invitation to an event from another iOS 5 user then it will appear in your 'Invitations' inbox, also accessible from the top-left corner.

Fig 1: Adding a new event is a simple process. Enter its details, start/end times, whether it's repeated and add invitees if you wish

# "You can choose to repeat the event every day, week, fortnight, month or year"

## Schedule appointments

The Calendar app is a great way to organise your life as you can effortlessly schedule appointments on the fly and invite other people to attend straight from the app. To schedule an appointment, either press and hold on a time slot directly on your calendar, or tap the '+' button in the bottom-right corner. An event note will then be placed at that time and a floating box will appear, into which you can enter all of the details (Fig 1).

Start by giving your event a title and a location and then tap on the start date and time to access a handy slider system that you can use to adjust the day, date and time down to five-minute intervals (Fig 2). If the event is set to take place regularly, you can choose to repeat it every day, week, fortnight, month or year, plus you can also get the app to alert you when the event is about to start. Once all of the details have been entered, tap on the 'Invitees' section and then start selecting people from your Contacts app, which is integrated into the Calendar app. Tap 'Done' when you are happy with everything and bear in mind that you can make adjustments to the details at any time by tapping on the event in your calendar and then tapping 'Edit'.

Fig 2: Set the start and end times for your event by using the sliders at the bottom

Fig 3: You can add an event direct from all views, except Year

## Create an event

Schedule an event simply by tapping the screen

### 1: Tap on a time

Press and hold on a time slot on the page on which you wish to schedule.

### 2: Enter details

Enter a title for your event and a location in the floating window that appears.

### 3: Enter start/end time

Tap on the start time and then move the sliders to set the start and end time.

### 4: Invite attendees

Tap 'Add Invitees' and then invite people to attend from your Contacts.

# Calendar

**Calendar views**
You can view your calendar by Day, Week, Month, Year or List by tapping the respective tabs at the top of the window

**Your calendar**
The current day and date will be displayed in the top-left corner. You can tap on a date on the calendar to jump straight to that particular day

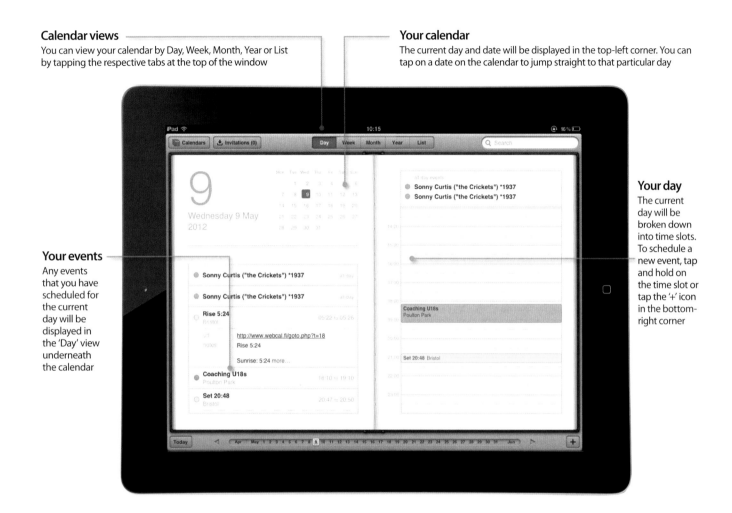

**Your day**
The current day will be broken down into time slots. To schedule a new event, tap and hold on the time slot or tap the '+' icon in the bottom-right corner

**Your events**
Any events that you have scheduled for the current day will be displayed in the 'Day' view underneath the calendar

## Changeable views

Depending on how much you like to plan ahead, you can view your calendar by Day, Week, Month, Year or List, simply by tapping the respective tab at the top of the window. This makes it easier to see your various appointments and key dates going forward.

The Day view lists all of your current appointments for the day by a page divided into time slots. You can scroll up and down to schedule appointments through the entire day and those that you have currently scheduled will be listed on the left-hand page beneath the calendar. The Week view loses the in-depth data displayed in your list of appointments, but it provides an at-a-glance overview of all of the events you have scheduled for the coming week. The Month view (Fig 1) cuts back on more detail, but allows you to gaze and plan further into the future, as does the Year view (Fig 2), which simply highlights the key dates you have planned in. The List view (Fig 3) prioritises your appointments by providing one long scrollable list on the left-hand page that you can swipe down through to see all of the forthcoming events that you've scheduled.

*Fig 1: The Month view provides an overview of every event that you have scheduled for the forthcoming month*

*Fig 2: The Year view lacks the level of detail of others, but all key dates are colour-coded to make it easy to see what's coming up*

*Fig 3: The List view focuses on your events, which you can scroll down through via the left-hand column*

Fig 1: You can assign key dates to contacts by tapping 'Edit', then selecting 'add field' and choosing 'Birthday' or 'Date'

# "It's a great system that ensures you never miss an important birthday or anniversary"

## Sync birthdays and anniversaries from Contacts

The best thing about default iOS apps is the way in which they all work seamlessly together behind the scenes to make your life easier. This is especially evident with the Calendar and Contacts apps, because if you assign key dates such as birthdays and anniversaries to people in your Contacts app, they will automatically appear on the respective dates in your Calendar app.

To add and assign key dates to Contacts, find the relevant contact in your Contacts app database, tap 'Edit' and then scroll down until you find the option called 'add field'. Tap this and then scroll down until you see the options called 'Birthday' and 'Date' (Fig 1). Tap one of these and add a birthday field and an anniversary field respectively to your contact sheet. Tap these new options on the contact sheet and then assign the correct date before tapping 'Done' to conclude the editing (Fig 2). Now launch your Calendar app and go to the date in question to see that the details have now automatically been assigned to that date (Fig 3). It's a great system that ensures you never miss an important birthday or an even more important anniversary. Magic!

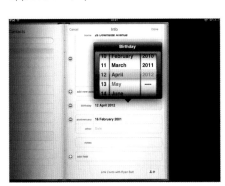

Fig 2: Enter those important dates and they will be saved when you tap on the 'Done' button

Fig 3: All of the key dates will then instantly be synced to your Calendar and appear on the respective days

## Use iCloud syncing
Ensure all of your iOS devices are using the same calendar

### 1: Launch Settings
To start syncing, launch the Settings app from your Home screen.

### 2: Tap on iCloud
Next, tap the 'iCloud' section from the list on the left.

### 3: Log in
Ensure you're logged into the same iCloud account as your other devices.

### 4: Turn on Calendar
Move the 'Calendars' slider to the 'On' position and everything will be synced.

## Set event alerts
### Get notified when an important event is looming

### 1: Create an event
Press and hold to create a new event or select 'Edit' on an existing event.

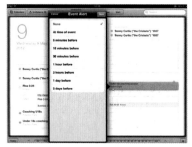

### 2: Tap Alert
Scroll down the floating details box and tap on the 'Alert' section.

### 3: Select period
Now choose how far ahead of the event you wish to be reminded.

### 4: Get alerted
Your iPad will now alert you at the preset time in the run-up to the event.

## Your calendars
Once iCloud syncing across devices has been activated, you can tap on the 'Calendars' button in Calendar to toggle all of your calendars on or off

## Activate or deactivate
You can turn your various calendars on or off simply by tapping on the name of the calendar in the list provided

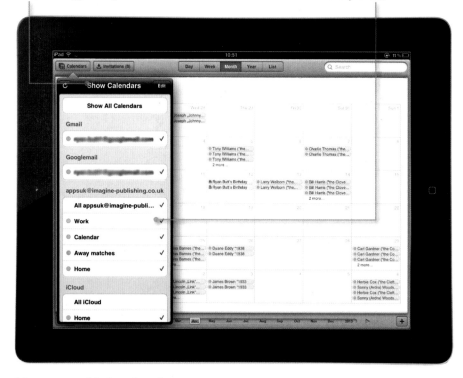

## Manage multiple calendars
One of the best features of the Calendar app is the way in which you can manage and merge multiple calendars at the same time. For example, you may have one calendar that is specific to work events and dates, one for personal events and dates, and another for recreational events and dates. These calendars can be colour-coded so that you can see, at a glance, what type of events are scheduled for the current day and you can turn them on or off at will so that your main calendar only displays what you want it to.

When creating new calendar events, you can tap on the 'Calendar' option in the floating window (Fig 1) to assign which type of calendar your event applies to and then tap the 'Calendars' button in the top-left corner of the screen to view all of your active calendars. The list will display all calendars, including those synced from your Mac or iPhone, provided that you have the Calendar option under the 'iCloud' section in Settings turned on. From the list, you can tap on a calendar to turn it off or on to determine the information that is displayed within your main calendar (Fig 2). So if, for instance, you only want to see which work events you have scheduled, then you would tap on all of the other calendars in the list to temporarily deactivate them.

*Fig 1: When setting an event, tap on the 'Calendar' option to determine which calendar the event applies to*

*Fig 2: Tap the 'Calendars' button in the top-left corner to see all calendars and turn them on or off*

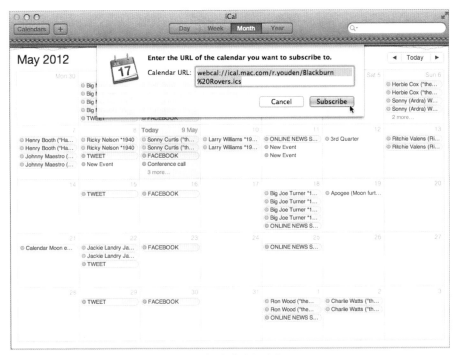

*Fig 1: Search for iCal files on the internet, click on the link and then hit the 'Subscribe' button*

# "You can even use iCal to subscribe to calendars published on the internet"

## Sync with third-party calendars

In your Mac's iCal app, you can create calendars to keep track of all sorts of activities, such as your work meetings, your spouse's meetings, after-school activities for the kids, family birthdays and so on. You can even use iCal to subscribe to calendars published on the internet. Let's say your kids' soccer league publishes the practice and match schedules on the league's site. To subscribe, click on the 'Calendar' drop-down menu in iCal and then choose 'Subscribe' (Fig 1). Next, type in the URL for the website where the schedule is published and then check the 'Refresh' checkbox to have iCal automatically update

your copy of the calendar when updates are published. Finally, click the 'Subscribe' button to get the calendar merged with your existing calendars. You can find plenty of novel iCal files by searching the internet and, in most cases, the setup will be done for you just by clicking on the relevant link on the website.

Once you've subscribed to the ones you want, ensure that your Mac and iPad are connected to the same iCloud account and your new iCal calendars will then be synced with your iPad and will magically appear in the list of active calendars that is displayed by tapping the 'Calendars' button in the top-left corner of the screen (Fig 3).

*Fig 2: You can make slight adjustments, such as colour-coding the calendar for easy reference*

*Fig 3: The new iCal files will then be synced, via your iCloud, back to your iPad*

## Search for events
### Find events in your busy schedule easily by searching

### 1: Tap Search
Start the process by tapping the search field in the top-right corner.

### 2: Enter keywords
Use the keyboard to type in keywords to narrow the search.

### 3: Scroll list
Swipe up or down to move through the list of possibilities provided.

### 4: Tap an event
When you see the event in question, tap on it in the list.

# Clock

With iOS 6, we were greeted with a completely new Clock app on the iPad.
Here's a look at the features this new app offers

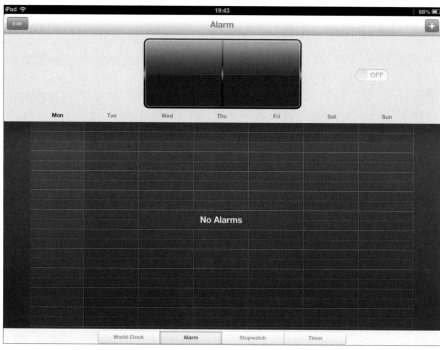

## Use it to:

- **The World clock**
  Check the times for multiple cities at a glance.

- **Daily alarms**
  You can create as many alarms as you need to.

- **Stopwatch**
  Never worry about timing your laps again.

- **Timers**
  Set a timer from one minute to one day.

- **Sounds**
  A myriad of alarm sounds as well as your iTunes library.

*Fig 1 (top left): In Clock, Alarm options are intuitive and very easy to understand*

*Fig 2 (bottom left): Repeating alarms helps you conveniently create multiple new alerts*

*Fig 3 (main image): The main screen allows you to organise your week ahead*

# Set alarms and use the timer

## Clock is an intuitive and resourceful multipurpose app

### Set an alarm

When you first look at the alarm screen, which can be reached by tapping the 'Alarm' icon at the bottom of the screen, you are presented with a blank interface that offers little instruction, as shown in the first image. When you tap the '+' icon in the top right-hand corner, a small screen pops up with multiple options. Choose the time you want to set the alarm for using the scroll wheels at the bottom and then give the alarm a name in the 'Label' field. You can choose from a number of sounds for your alarm and even select songs directly from your iTunes library.

As you can see in the second image, the familiar layout is perfectly clear and needs almost no introduction. One box that deserves a mention is the 'Repeat' option which will prove to be extremely useful over time. When you tap it, a new panel will appear that lets you choose when you want to set your alarms for. You can choose as many options as you wish. This is particularly useful for different alarm times and to remind you about meetings and appointments that occur at irregular intervals or things you need reminding for that you don't do everyday. All your alarm needs are catered for with this app.

*Fig 1: The Stopwatch screen is designed to be easy to use when accurate timings are required*

# "Display multiple laps at a time using the Stopwatch function"

## Use Stopwatch and Timer

There is more to the iPad Clock app than just setting alarms and telling the time. You can use the Stopwatch facility to keep track of any activity which involves accurate timing. Tap the 'Stopwatch' icon at the bottom and you will be presented with a screen showing two buttons at the top and a number in the centre, as shown in the first image. When you tap the start button, the clock will start timing. Tap the same button, which now shows 'Lap' on it, and you can start timing all over again, with the exact time of the first lap noted. This is shown in the second image and the same

process can be repeated as many times as you like. Simply press 'Stop' when you are done.

To use the Timer, tap the 'Timer' icon at the bottom. You can now use the scroll wheels in the centre (see the third image) to choose the exact length of time you need it to run for. The maximum time is 24 hours, but you can break this down to within a minute. This functionality is ideal for cooking, sessions at the gym and other activities where you always need precise timing. You can pause the timer at any time with the 'Pause' icon in the top-right or click 'Done' on the left, during a countdown, to cancel it ahead of schedule.

*Fig 2: You can time as many laps as you like using the large buttons at the top of the screen.*

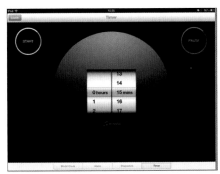

*Fig 3: The Timer is especially useful for cooking and other activities that are time-dependant.*

## Add world clocks
### Keep track of times in multiple cities

### 1: Use the icons at the top
Tap one of the clocks at the top of the screen to get started.

### 2: Choose a preferred city
A list will appear when you tap a clock. Choose a city you want to add.

### 3: Multiple cities
It will now display times and weather symbols of the cities on the map.

### 4: Remove/Add new cities
Tap 'Edit' (top-left) to delete a clock. Repeat steps 1 to 3 to add new ones.

# Contacts

Keep track of everyone you know with Apple's intuitive digital contacts database. Keep in touch with just a few simple taps

## Use it to:

- **Add contacts**
  Create a new contacts card for everyone you know.

- **Include detail**
  Enter even the most intricate details.

- **Share contacts**
  Contact info can be shared or received via email or SMS.

- **Integrate apps**
  Get essential info directly from Notes and Maps apps.

- **Add photos**
  Assign a face to a contact from your Photos app.

- **Search**
  Find what you're looking for.

- **Group contacts**
  Group contacts together to speed up navigation.

*Fig 1 (top left): The 'Add Field' section lets you apply even greater detail to any of your contacts*

*Fig 2 (bottom left): Assign images from Photos to any contact by tapping on the picture frame*

*Fig 3 (main image): Tap '+' to add a new contact and fill in all of the details that you know into the fields*

# Manage your contacts

We guide you around Apple's intuitive contacts database app and show you how to make friends and influence people

## Add contacts

The Contacts app is far more than just a straightforward digital phone book. You can store pretty much anything you know about anyone within its intuitive interface, including IM addresses, birthdays, anniversaries and websites, as well as the names and numbers. You can also put a photo to a name, add email addresses (so as to be able to send a message with a tap), add notes and important dates to any contact and assign FaceTime info to make video calls straight from the Contacts app.

To add a new contact, tap the '+' icon at the bottom of the screen and then start assigning the information that you know in the respective fields (Fig 3). The amount of info that you can include is staggering. Once you have filled in the main fields, scroll down and you'll see a section called 'Add Field'. Tap on this and you'll be presented with a drop-down menu crammed with yet more options relating to info that you can assign to any contact (Fig 1). These include Twitter tags, birthdays and related people – so you can link contacts together. To assign a photo to a contact, tap on the 'add photo' box at the top and pick an image from your Photos app (Fig 2). Check that all of the information you have entered is correct and then tap 'Done' to add your new contact to your database.

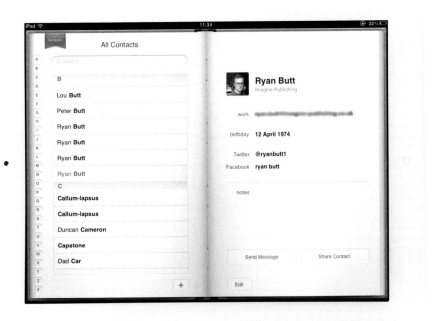

## Add a photo
Put a face to the name by
assigning photos to contacts

### 1: Create new contact
While in your Contacts app, tap the '+'
icon to create a new contact.

### 2: Tap frame
Tap the picture frame icon at the top of
your new contact page.

### 3: Choose photo
Pick a suitable image from the ones
saved in your Photos app.

### 4: Use photo
Move and scale the image and then tap
'Use' to complete the process.

*Fig 1: Tap 'Share Contact', then choose
whether to send it via email or message*

# "You can quickly email or message out your contact cards to other people"

## Share a contact

The better you know a person, the more
details can be entered into the Contacts app
to keep track of them. And due to the sheer
volume of information that you can enter
when creating a new contact, the process
can be a little time-consuming. However, by
sharing contacts, you can then quickly email
or message out your contact cards to other
people or get them sent straight to you, by
other people, directly on your iPad.

To share a contact with other people, simply
tap the 'Share Contact' button at the bottom
of a contact page and then choose to either
email it or send it as a message from within
the app (Fig 1). When receiving contacts
from other people, which will come via the
Messages app or email, simply tap on the VCF
file attachment and then you will see options
to 'Create New Contact' or 'Add to Existing
Contact' (Fig 3). If you choose the former then
the information received from the VCF file will
be placed in the relevant fields within a new
contacts card. You can fill in any additional info
at this point, and then tap 'Done' to add the
new contact to your database.

*Fig 2: Whatever method you use to share the contact, it will be
added as a VCF attachment*

*Fig 3: When receiving a contact, tap on the VCF attachment and
use the info to create a new contact*

# Contacts

## Your contacts
The names of all of your contacts will be listed alphabetically on the left-hand page. Tap on a letter for speedy navigation

## Contact groups
You can group contacts together to make it easier to find people. Tap the 'Groups' ribbon and then tap on a category

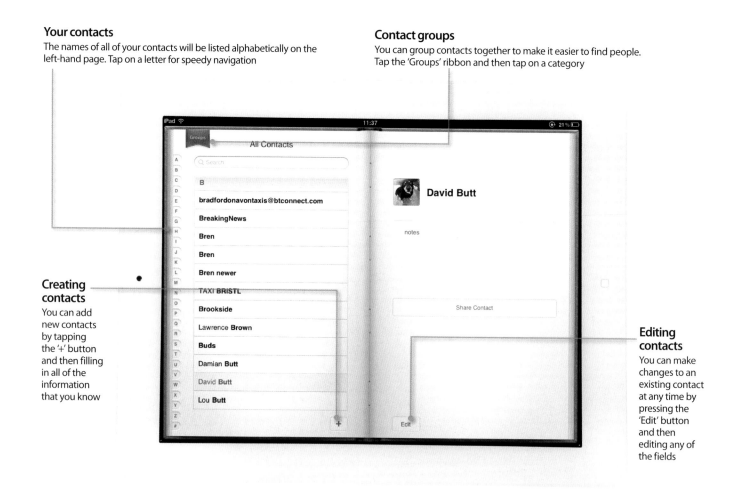

## Creating contacts
You can add new contacts by tapping the '+' button and then filling in all of the information that you know

## Editing contacts
You can make changes to an existing contact at any time by pressing the 'Edit' button and then editing any of the fields

## Maps/Notes integration
One of the many bonuses of the default apps on your iPad is that they all work together to make your life easier. A good example is the ability to gather and assign essential contact info from the Notes and Maps apps.

For example, if you type an address or a phone number into your Notes app, when you banish the keyboard, the details will become underlined on the page (Fig 1) and you'll be able to tap and hold on it to bring up a floating menu of options, including 'Open in Maps' and 'Add to Contacts'. If you choose the second option, two further options will allow you to 'Create New Contact' or 'Add to Existing Contact' (see Fig 2), after which you'll be back to the familiar Contacts app interface where you can enter any additional info before storing the contact. You can also get addresses

added to your contacts from the Maps app. In this case, you simply need to find the relevant location on the map and then drop a pin into position to mark it. Next, tap on the blue 'i' icon and you will see the option to 'Add to Contacts' at the bottom of the information window (Fig 3). Tap this and the now familiar options that proceed will allow you to assign the location to any of your contacts.

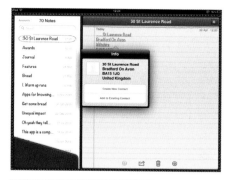

*Fig 2 (right): You can use the info to create a new contact or simply add it to an existing one*

## "Gather and assign essential contact info from the Notes and Maps apps"

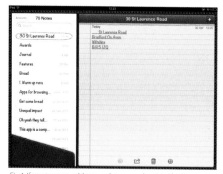

*Fig 1: If you type an address or phone number into the Notes app, it will become underlined and you'll be able to add it to Contacts*

*Fig 3: You can also use addresses to assign to contacts straight from the Maps app*

## Add extra information

As we have already explored, the sheer volume of information that you can assign to your contacts is staggering and even the most intricate of details – such as birthdays and anniversaries – can be added in just a few simple taps (Fig 2).

When creating a new contact, enter all of the obvious info such as names and phone numbers, then scroll down to the bottom of the card, where you'll see the option called 'Add Field' (Fig 3). Tap on this to bring up a floating menu packed full of options to assign additional info. These include options to include all aspects of the person's name (including prefix, phonetic first and last names, suffix and nickname), their job title and department, Twitter tag, birthday and related people. Every time you tap on a new field, it will be added to the main contact card and you'll be able to enter the info that you know. Some fields also have multiple levels connected to them – such as 'Profile' (Fig 1). Tap on this and the field to enter a Facebook profile address to be added, then a Flickr account, then LinkedIn, then MySpace – so an entire galaxy of social networking details can also be quickly assigned.

## "The sheer volume of information that you can assign to your contacts is staggering"

Fig 1: The 'Profile' option allows you to add details of the various social networking services

Fig 2: You can even assign birthdays and add your own notes to a particular contact

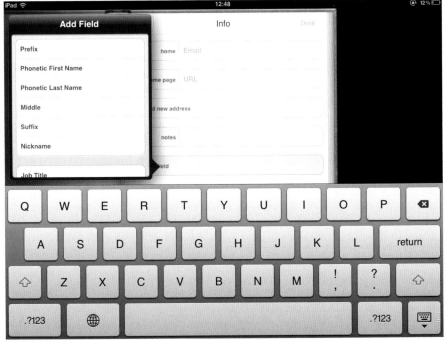
Fig 3: When creating a new contacts card, tap on 'Add Field' to expand your options

## Send a contact
### Share your contacts quickly and easily with others

### 1: Share contact
In Contacts, tap the 'Share Contact' button at the bottom of the page.

### 2: Choose option
Now choose whether to attach the contact to an email or message.

### 3: Via email
If emailing, your contact card will be attached as a VCF file.

### 4: Via message
Enter the email address or iPhone number of the recipient and hit 'Send'.

# Messages

Discover how to send unlimited text messages to other iOS devices absolutely free

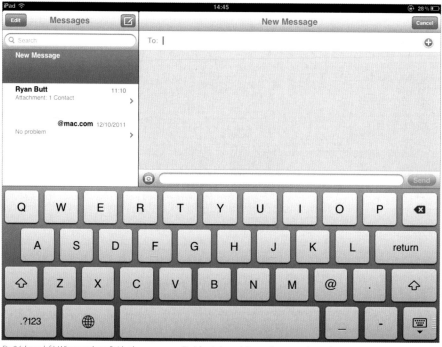

*Fig 1 (above): The conversation will open up its own window where all sent and received messages can be viewed*

*Fig 2 (above-left): When you have finished writing your message, hit 'Send' to fire it off*

*Fig 3 (main image): Tap on the pen and paper icon to create a new message, then enter the registered email address or iPhone number of the recipient*

## Use it to:

- **Send messages**
  Send unlimited free text messages to other iOS device users.

- **Attach photos**
  Attach images within the Messages app or from the Photos app.

- **Share contacts**
  Contact info can be shared or received via email or SMS.

- **Integrate apps**
  Get essential information directly from the Notes and Maps apps.

- **Message groups**
  Text messages to groups you have assigned in your Contacts app.

- **Quick confirmation**
  Get confirming that your messages have been read.

# Send texts on iPad

We guide you around Apple's quick and easy text messaging service and showcase its many convenient features

### Text using iMessage

When iMessage was revealed as a new addition to the iPad's arsenal of apps, it was an exciting moment because it allows users to send and receive unlimited text messages, via Wi-Fi or 3G, from any iOS device.

The iMessage app, which is familiar to millions of iPhone users, is built in to the iPad's new Messages app so you can send texts, photos, videos, locations and contacts, keep everyone in the loop with group messaging, track your messages with delivery receipts and optional read receipts, and even start a text conversation on one device and then pick up where you left off on another (Fig 1).

To text using the Messages app, open it from the home screen, tap on the pen and paper icon at the top of the interface, and then enter the email address (Apple ID or another one registered with the iMessage service) or iPhone number of the person you wish to send the message to (Fig 3). Then tap on the text field and use the keyboard to input your message. At this point, you can tap the camera icon to attach an image from your Photos app; otherwise, if you are good to go, hit the 'Send' button to fire off your message to its intended recipient (Fig 2). A new window will then show all correspondence between you and that particular iOS user.

*Fig 1: You can share photos via message attachments straight from within the Photos app*

## Send photos, locations and contacts via Messages

Like all of the other built-in iOS apps, Messages is integrated into the other communicative-style apps too. It is easy to attach a photo to your texts within the Messages app by tapping the camera icon that's visible next to the text window while composing a message. However, you may find that, it sometimes is far more convenient to get your message across while you're in other apps.

For example, while looking at images in the Photos app, if the urge to share one of your pictures takes over then you can simply tap the sharing icon in the top-right corner and choose to share the image via the 'Message' option (see Fig 1 above).

Likewise, you can share locations with contacts from within the Maps app by pinpointing a location and then tapping on the blue 'i' icon (Fig 2). You will be presented with a floating box that relates to the location, at the bottom of which is the option to 'Share Location' (via email, message or tweet).

Finally, as we have already explored in the Contacts guide, you can also share contact details via the Messages service. Just go to the relevant contact in your database and then tap on the 'Share Contact' button at the bottom of the page. From the floating menu that appears, you will be able to choose the 'Message' option and then instantly attach the VCF file to an outgoing message to send that contact card to the recipient (Fig 3).

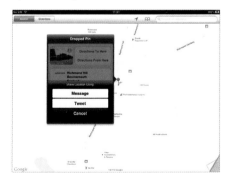

*Fig 2: You can share locations that you pinpoint in Maps, via message or tweet (a Twitter account is needed)*

*Fig 3: Sharing contacts via Message is a quick and easy way to expand your database*

## Delete messages
### It's easy to erase certain parts of a conversation

### 1: Go to window
Open the messaging window of the conversation you wish to edit.

### 2: Tap share icon
To start editing, tap the sharing icon in the top-right corner.

### 3: Tick boxes
Tap the circle next to each message to place a tick next to it.

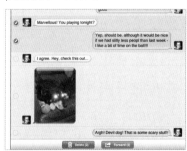

### 4: Delete messages
With the messages selected, tap 'Delete' at the bottom of the window.

## Your messages

Messages will be assigned to specific contacts. Tap on a contact to reveal a window displaying all message correspondence between parties

## Forward or delete

Tap the sharing icon in the top-right corner to select individual messages to either delete or forward to other contacts

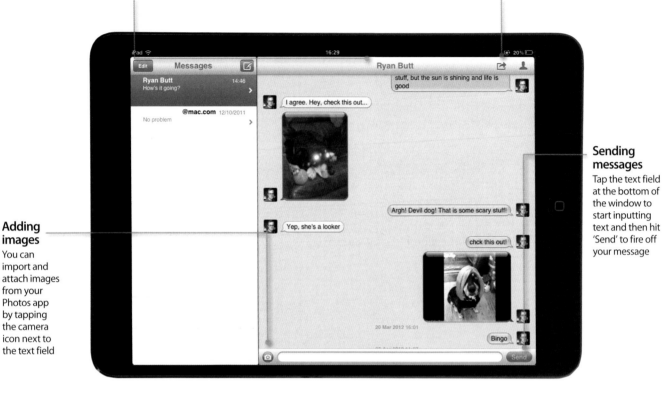

## Sending messages

Tap the text field at the bottom of the window to start inputting text and then hit 'Send' to fire off your message

## Adding images

You can import and attach images from your Photos app by tapping the camera icon next to the text field

## Group messaging

As the Messages app works in harmony with your Contacts app, you can access the same groups that you create in Contacts and send out one message to all of them at the same time. This is especially handy when, for example, you are working remotely and need feedback from your colleagues. Or you're organising a party and you want to keep all the guests in the loop without having to message each one individually.

When creating a new message, tap the blue '+' icon next to the recipient field (Fig 1) and a floating window will be displayed that shows all of your contacts. From this menu, tap 'Groups' in the top-left corner and then pick the group from the list provided (Fig 2). Once you have selected a group, all of the members will be added to the 'To' field and all correspondence between everyone in that group will be displayed in the same window (Fig 3), making it easy to monitor the conversation and everyone's respective comments. You will be alerted as usual whenever a member of the group chips in, and you can delete or forward messages from within the window as you normally do.

## "You can access the groups you create in Contacts and send out one message to all of them at the same time"

Fig 1: Tap the blue '+' icon while creating a new message to add Contacts groups to your message list

Fig 2: Tap on the 'Groups' button to choose a group of people that you have created in the Contacts app

Fig 3: Tap on a group to add everyone in that group as recipients to your message

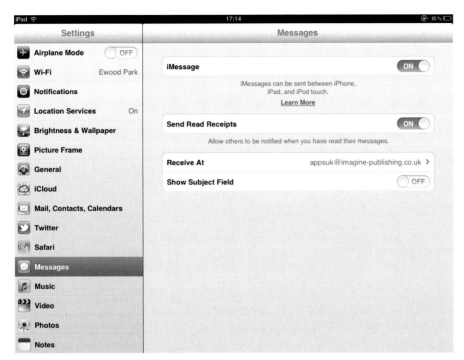

*Fig 1: Go to Settings and activate the 'Send Read Receipts' option in the Messages section*

*Fig 2: When a message has been delivered, it will notify you under their picture*

*Fig 3: This word will change to 'Read' when the recipient opens the message on their device*

# "A special setting tells you if and when a particular message has been read"

## Read/delivery receipts

When you send messages via the Messages app, it is important to know that they actually make it through to their intended recipients. Thankfully, whenever you send a message, you will receive a time stamp (which will appear above each message) so that you know it has been delivered at a certain time on a certain date.

You can even activate a special setting that tells you if and when a particular message has been read, which is useful for clarifying details on group events and suchlike. To activate this feature, launch your Settings app from the Home screen and then tap on the 'Messages' category from the list down the left-hand side. Here you will see an option called 'Send Read Receipts'. Activate this by moving the slider to 'On' (Fig 1). Now whenever you send a message, the word 'Delivered' will appear under the recipient (Fig 2). When the recipient reads the messages, the word will change to 'Read' alongside the time at which it was read, making it easy to check whether your messages have been received and understood by all concerned (Fig 3). It's a very useful service that makes communicating via text messages as intuitive as possible.

## Multiple addresses
### Add extra email addresses to ensure you get the message

### 1: Launch Settings
Launch your Settings app and then go to the 'Messages' section.

### 2: Tap on 'Receive At'
When in the Messages settings, tap on the 'Receive At' option.

### 3: Add another email
Now tap on 'Add Another Email…' and type in a new address.

### 4: Remove addresses
To remove an email address, tap on it and then choose 'Remove This Email'.

# Reminders

When you think to yourself, "I don't need to write that down, I'll remember it", it's a sure-fire guarantee that you won't, but help is at hand with Reminders

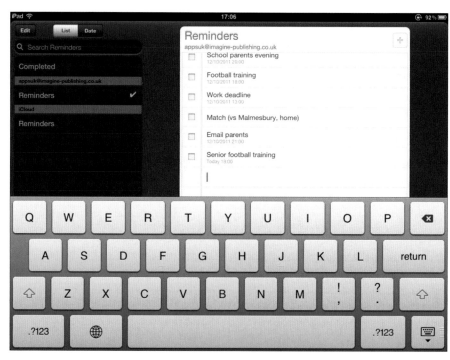

## Use it to:

- **Set tasks**
  Make quick and easy to-do lists for yourself.

- **Set deadlines**
  Set dates and times for when the tasks need to be completed.

- **Get alerts**
  The app will notify you when a deadline looms.

- **Tick them off**
  A tick-list format makes it easy to mark off tasks as they're completed.

- **Work with iCloud**
  Make lists on any Apple devices and access them all from your iPad.

# Never forget with Reminders

## Use this simple app to set and schedule tasks for yourself

*Fig 1 (top left): You can set the app to remind you to complete tasks on certain days and times*

*Fig 2 (bottom left): You can view your tasks by tapping on the days of the calendar*

*Fig 3 (main image): Tap the '+' to create new tasks and reminders*

### Exploring the interface

The Reminders app lets you organise your life into to-do lists, complete with due dates and locations, and the app also works with iCal, Outlook and iCloud, so any changes you make will automatically update on all of your devices and calendars. The Reminders interface is very simple. The main section is presented as a notebook page and you can add reminders by tapping the '+' button in the top-right corner of the screen (Fig 3). Each reminder that you set will be presented as a list with a tickbox next to it. When you complete a task, you place a tick in the box and it will be removed

from the list and placed in the 'Completed' section. Once a reminder has been set, you can tap on it in the list to edit it. This includes setting an alert so that the app will remind you about the task on a particular date and time. To do this, tap on the 'Remind Me' section, move the 'On a Day' slider to the 'On' position (Fig 1) and then tap on the date to change the day and time of the reminder.

When viewing your reminders, you can tap on the 'List' tab to view your current and completed reminders, and the 'Date' tab to view a handy calendar. Simply tap on a day to view the tasks you have set yourself (Fig 2).

Fig 1: Tap 'Edit' while in the List view to create fresh lists of tasks

# "If you create a task on one device, it will be synced across all of your devices"

## Create and manage multiple lists

Reminders is flexible enough to work how best you want it to. For example, you can create one long list of tasks and then assign due dates to each task, or you can create individual task lists for each day, making it easier to track what you need to do and what you have done. As we have mentioned, Reminders works with iCloud, so if you create a task on one device, it will be synced across all of your devices – including your Mac – so you don't have to worry about consulting different lists created on different devices. Tap on the 'List' tab in the top-left corner of the screen

and you'll be able to see all the reminders that you have set on your iPad and on other devices under the 'iCloud' section (ensure that the 'Reminders' slider is turned to 'On' in the iCloud section in Settings). You can also search for a task by entering keywords into the search field and create new lists by tapping the 'Edit' button (Figs 1&2).

By tapping the 'Date' tab, a calendar will be displayed down the side of the window and you'll be able to tap on specific days to assign tasks and view those that you have already set for that day (Fig 3), making it easy to turn every day into an epic win.

Fig 2: If you have lots of tasks on the go, you can enter keywords into the search field to find them

Fig 3: Tap on a calendar day to start assigning tasks to that particular day

## Add a reminder
If you have a deadline looming, set an alert

### 1: Tap on a task
Once you have created a task, tap on it in the list to bring up the details box.

### 2: Set to remind
Tap on the 'Remind Me' box and move the 'On a Day' slider to the 'On' position.

### 3: Tap on date
Tap the date under the slider and set a date and time to be reminded.

### 4: Get alerted
When the set alert time is reached, a push notification will remind you.

# Notes

You can take notes, make lists and jot down any thought quickly and easily with the Notes app. Here we guide you through some of its many features

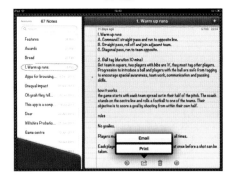

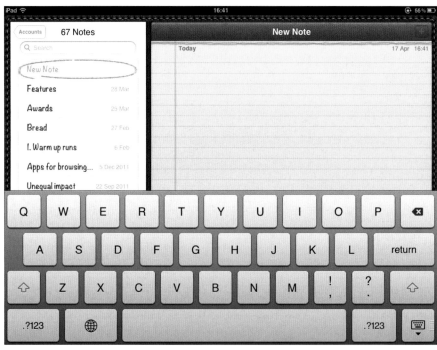

## Use it to:

- **Share your thoughts**
  You can email or print notes from within the app.

- **Save automatically**
  Your work will automatically be saved. Just close the app.

- **Sync with iCloud**
  Your notes can be synced across all of your devices.

- **Type quickly**
  You can launch the app in seconds in order to get typing quickly.

- **Organise automatically**
  All notes are categorised by the time and date created.

*Fig 1 (top left): By tapping the sharing icon you can print or email your notes straight from the app*

*Fig 2 (bottom left): Turn on the Notes iCloud feature in Settings to sync your notes across all devices*

*Fig 3 (main image): Tap the '+' icon to create a new note and start typing with the keyboard*

# Take notes with ease

Taking notes is simple with the iPad Notes app. Here's how it works

### Notes interface

The Notes app is the perfect way to quickly write down those ideas, lists and anything else that you may need to remember later on. The the app is serviced by an intuitive interface that places everything within the easy reach of the tap your fingers.

You can create a new note by tapping the '+' icon in the top-right corner of the screen and all of your notes are automatically stored, so there is no need to save what you write (Fig 3). Every note you create will be presented in an easily accessible list and anything you write down in the Notes app can be easily shared with others from within the app itself.

To start sharing your notes, tap the sharing icon that's located at the bottom of the screen (indicated by an arrow in a box) and you will be presented with options to Email or Print (Fig 1). If you opt to Email your note, the contents of the current note will be copied and pasted into an email. All you have to do then is add the recipient and you can mail it straight out from within the app without having to cut, paste and switch between apps yourself. If you have an AirPrint-enabled printer then you can also print your notes wirelessly. Notes is also iCloud compatible (Fig 2), so any notes you create can be accessed on all of your iOS devices and your Mac.

*Fig 1: Activate the caps lock in the Keyboard Settings and then double-tap the shift key to utilise it*

# "Press and hold the numbers key, and slide your finger to the number you want"

## Keyboard tricks

If you use Notes regularly then you'll be well used to the iPad's keyboard – but there are plenty of tricks and shortcuts. For example, pressing the space bar twice in quick succession will automatically place a full stop and a space at the end of your sentence. If you also loathe the way that you have to switch to a number keyboard just to type one number or symbol then simply press and hold on the numbers key, and quickly slide your finger to the number or symbol you wish to place before taking your finger off the keyboard – it

will switch back to the default letters keyboard, allowing you to continue typing.

If you like to type in capitals then you can enable a caps lock in the Keyboard section of the General Settings and then activate it by double-tapping the Shift key (Fig 1). When typing with proper punctuation, you can utilise a handy shortcut to add an apostrophe by holding your finger on the '!' key (Fig 2). An apostrophe key will then appear that you can slide up to type, saving you the time it would take to switch keyboards. Letters like 'E' and 'I' can be held down for accents (Fig 3).

*Fig 2: For a quick apostrophe, hold down the 'I' key and slide your finger up*

*Fig 3: Holding your finger on various other keys, such as 'E' and 'I', will provide accents*

## Add a note
### How to add new pages to your virtual notebook

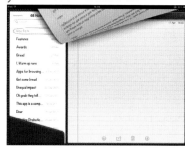

### 1: Tap to add
Tap the '+' icon in the top-right corner to create a new note.

### 2: Start typing
Start typing with the keyboard and the first words will form the title of the note.

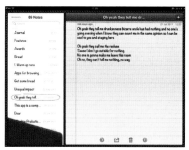

### 3: Cycle through notes
Cycle through your notes by pressing the arrows at the bottom of the screen.

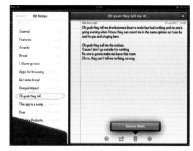

### 4: Delete notes
Delete notes by tapping the trash can icon at the bottom of the screen.

# Maps

Maps can work as your main digital map, your navigation service and a source of interest all in one. It's time to learn how it all comes together

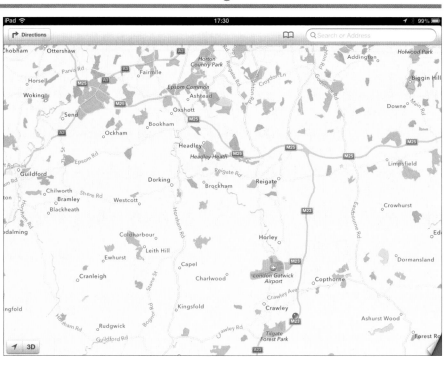

## Use it to:

- **Navigation**
  Turn-by-turn navigation lets you navigate in style.

- **Traffic**
  Check the traffic as you drive to avoid any delays.

- **Flyover**
  Explore the world using the beautiful 3D flyovers.

- **Local search**
  Find places near you with a couple of taps.

- **Names**
  Street and place names highlight their detail.

- **Siri**
  Use Siri with Maps for hands-free exploring.

*Fig 1 (top left): You can manipulate the look of the map using the icons*

*Fig 2 (main image): The main Maps interface is very simple and easy to understand immediately*

*Fig 3 (bottom left): Directions are extremely quick to set up and work perfectly if you are in a hurry*

# Find your way with Maps

There is a lot to explore in Maps and we will help you understand every feature

## Maps in iOS 6

The Maps interface is very simple and should pose no problems once you know where everything is. When you start the app, you will see a map in the middle of the screen and some minimalist indicators around it. These are shown in the first image. If you tap the bottom right-hand corner, which looks like a slightly turned page, you will see a set of icons appear. These are detailed in the second image. On the opposite side (top-left), you will see an icon marked 'Directions'. Simply tap this and a search bar will appear for you to input a destination and starting point for your journey,

as shown in the third image. On the main map, you will see that the colours have been carefully chosen to make the important details stand out. Airports and other facilities will be coloured purple, larger roads, yellow, and parks in green. This helps to offer an immediate and familiar view of the area you are looking at and works very well even though the graphics have a slight cartoony look to them. Finally, you can use the search bar (top-right) to quickly find a location by simply typing a name or address. It will immediately find the best result for your search terms and jump to it on the main map.

Fig 1: Entering locations to navigate to takes a couple of seconds and the software will do the rest for you

# "Choose the fastest route for your destination from the three routes offered"

## Turn-by-turn navigation

The inclusion of turn-by-turn navigation in Maps offers a huge bonus for iPad users because it is an extremely useful facility. To start the process, tap the 'Directions' icon and then enter a postcode or name of a location. Notice that your current location is already shown in the top panel which is highlighted in the first image. Tap the 'Route' icon and Maps will work out the full route in seconds and present it on the map (see the second image). Notice that three routes are offered and all you need to do is select the one you

prefer to follow. As you tap each route, the time and distance will be shown at the top of the screen to help you. Now tap 'Start' and the first instruction will be shown top-right (see the third image). If you tap the small '3D' icon at the bottom, the view will change to a look that feels much more like traditional GPS navigation solutions. As you move, the instructions will change and so will the map, but the audible instructions mean that you can navigate without taking your eyes off the road for too long. It's a simple solution that works very efficiently.

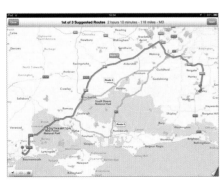

Fig 2: Three routes are always provided, giving you a choice between speed and distance

Fig 3: The 3D view is reminiscent of traditional navigation solutions and is very easy to follow

## Search a location
### Find useful information about any location

### 1: Use the search bar
Tap the search bar. Enter a location. Matches will appear immediately.

### 2: Choose a specific location
Choose a result and the map will immediately jump to your location.

### 3: Find more information
Some locations will have an 'i' icon on them. Tap it to see more information.

### 4: Work with the location
You can now share, bookmark or navigate to the location via the icons.

# Maps

## Use the icons
The icons can be tapped to display details about the location in question. It's a very useful extra feature.

## Lots of names
Street and location names make understanding any chosen map very easy. They also help navigating while walking.

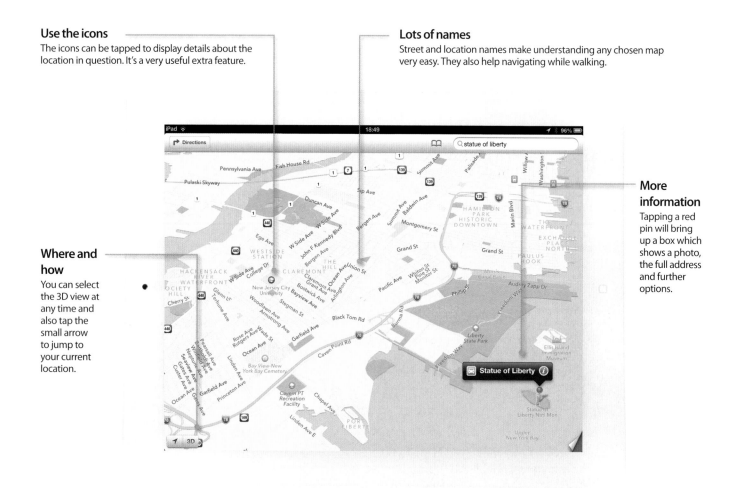

## More information
Tapping a red pin will bring up a box which shows a photo, the full address and further options.

## Where and how
You can select the 3D view at any time and also tap the small arrow to jump to your current location.

## Traffic

Finding places and navigating to them is great, but traffic is always a concern. Do not worry because Maps has an automatic traffic monitoring system built in, which you can use to set up for your journey in seconds. Tap the bottom-right icon and choose 'Show Traffic'. If there is traffic in the area you are viewing, it will be highlighted by small triangles which are shown in the first image. You will want to check the traffic when navigating, however, so after you have chosen a route, look for any triangles. Now tap one of them and you will see more information about the incident which includes the current delay time and how long the delay is expected to last, as shown in the second image. You may also see some roads marked with red dashes or amber dots (see third image). These dashes and dots indicate traffic delays with no specific cause apart from the number of cars on the road. All of this data is used when calculating your journey time and it is continually updated as you drive so you have a good, approximate idea of the how long it will take you to reach your destination. No traffic system is perfect, but once you know how it works, you will use it on every trip just to be sure you don't get stuck. Maps definitely makes travel less stressful.

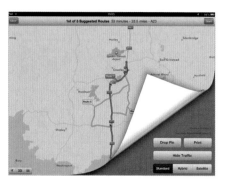

*Fig 1: Traffic problems are highlighted visually and are easy to recognise once you are used to them*

*Fig 2: Full traffic information for each incident is available with just one tap. It's accurate and works very efficiently*

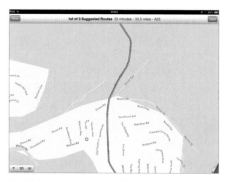

*Fig 3: Traffic is even detailed on smaller roads within cities so you can make the perfect routing choices*

Fig 1: The Satellite view is used to give you an aerial indication of what a building or location looks like

# "Spin around a location in Flyover by making a circle with your finger"

## Flyover

The Flyover feature in Maps is more of an interesting diversion than a serious tool, but it could prove useful if you are trying to find a particular building and need a first hand view of what it looks like. The first step is to search for a building, point of interest or location and to make sure that the 'Satellite' option is chosen from the icon in the bottom right-hand corner (see first image). The location will be shown on the map and you will see an icon with a building on it in the bottom left, if a Flyover view is available. Tap the icon and

the view will change, as shown in the second image. All that's left to do is to manipulate the image according to your preference. You can spin around a location by making a circle with your finger, pinch to zoom in and out and pan across larger areas by sliding your finger over the screen. The result is shown in the third image. As you can see, the level of detail is incredibly high and it really does make for an interesting way to explore the world around you. Take time to experiment with this feature and you will learn a lot about places you have never visited before.

Fig 2: The buildings icon will automatically take you to flyover mode which offers an enhanced 3D view

Fig 3: You can manipulate the view in any way you like by zooming, tilting and rotating with your fingers

## Add a bookmark
Bookmark multiple locations with ease

### 1: Find a location first
Enter a location in the top bar. You will be presented with a map and red pin.

### 2: Use the pin wisely
Tap the pin and a selection of options will appear. Select 'Add to Bookmarks'.

### 3: Name the new bookmark
Name the bookmark and then choose 'Save'. It will be added to your list.

### 4: Find all of your bookmarks
Tap the bookmark icon and a list will appear for you to select from.

## Print a map
### Print any location on a map in an instant

### 1: Print anywhere you want to
Find the location or area that you want to print and tap the page curl at the bottom.

### 2: A simple print box
Choose 'Print' and a box will appear with two boxes within it to manipulate.

### 3: One print. Multiple maps
Tap the '+' and '-' buttons to choose how many copies of the map you want to print.

### 4: Find the wireless printer
Choose 'Select Printer' and the iPad will find a compatible printer. Now tap 'Print'.

## Your own pins
When you drop a pin on the map, it will be displayed in purple so that you know it is one that you added.

## Full details
As much information as possible, including the nearest address, is shown for each PIN that you create.

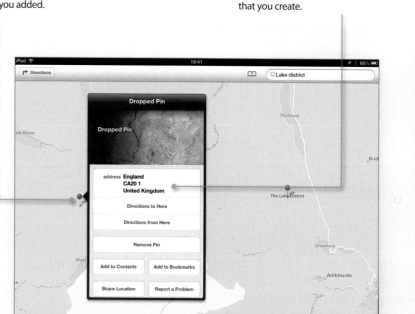

## Map styles
Depending on what you are searching for and the type of terrain shown, you may want to use different map styles for each area you find. When you are in a particular location, tap the page curl at the bottom and you will see options pop up which include Standard, Hybrid and Satellite which are shown in the first image. The standard view is a simplistic representation of the roads and points of interest within a particular area, but if you select 'Satellite', you will see much more detail on screen. As you can see in the second image, zooming in will help you to see everything in all of its glory and

the zoomed out view is merely useful as an overview. Selecting the 'Hybrid' option brings both views together and lets you see all of the street names on top of the realistic satellite view. This view is handy when trying to navigate while walking or for pinning down a particular street and then quickly seeing what it looks like, should you need to visit it. Icons are also shown in the hybrid view which can be tapped to bring up more information about a specific point of interest. It is good to know that there is always a view available that fits each individual location perfectly. Experiment with these views to familiarise yourself with their features.

Fig 1: You can choose between three map styles depending on your needs at the time

Fig 2: A huge amount of detail is included in the satellite view which is useful in many different ways

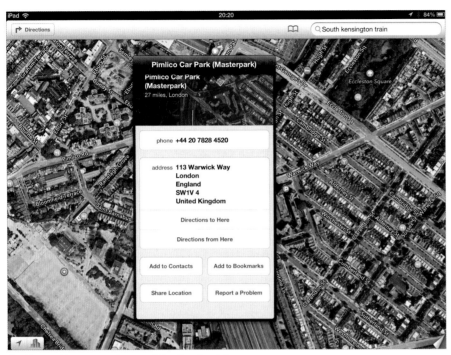

*Fig 1: You can add a new contact from a specific location with only three taps*

# "Contacts and Maps work in perfect harmony to speed up your routine"

## Contacts integration

The contacts integration is particularly useful in Maps and can be used in a variety of ways. When you have found a location, tap the 'i' and the box will appear with all of the options available to you including 'Add to Contacts'. This is shown in the first image. Tap 'Add to contacts' and a new box will appear asking if you want to create a new contact or add the address to an existing one (see second image). Choose one and the contacts panel will appear. Complete the details you want to include, tap 'Done' and your new contact will be saved for you to use later. That is all you have to do to create a new contact with

accurate map data. But the real beauty of the system will become clear later on when you need to use the information you have saved. The next time you tap address in Contacts, the Maps app will pop up on screen with the location you have entered already displayed. You can now choose 'Directions to here' to navigate from your location to the address of your contact. Contacts and Apple Maps work in perfect harmony and they will speed up your daily routine by a great deal. Maps is another genius way of Apple products syncing data from different apps to give you the best user experience possible and help make navigation an easy affair.

*Fig 2: You can add locations to existing contacts or create new ones based around them*

*Fig 3: The addresses in your contacts will be automatically linked to Apple Maps for quick navigation*

## Share a location
### Share locations with anyone using Maps

### 1: Find the share button
Tap the 'i' on any location and then choose 'Share Location'.

### 2: Select delivery method
Choose if you want to send the location by email, message, Twitter or Facebook.

### 3: Complete sharing
Add a description and then send the message to complete the process.

### 4: Dealing with shared data
When tapped, the data will open Maps or display information.

# Facebook

Hot on the heels of Twitter, Facebook now finds itself integrated and ready to use on your iPad. Here's how it'll change your iOS 6 life and make it easier than ever

## Use it to:

- **Post a status in seconds**
  The new Notification Center shortcuts make status updates snappy.

- **Share your content from any app**
  Show friends content with iOS 6 Share Sheets.

- **Keep all contacts up to date**
  Sync profile photos, emails and phone numbers.

- **Stay on top of events**
  See birthdays, parties and more in Calendar.

- **Share your favourite apps with friends**
  Like apps in Apple's App Store or in iTunes.

# Sync Facebook with your iPad

### Sync your favourite social network for better optimisation

*Fig 1 (top left): To link your Facebook account, simply enter your login credentials in the Settings app*

*Fig 2 (bottom left): Share sheets appear but they are the quickest from Notification Center*

*Fig 3 (main image): Add links to your status posts from Safari and Photos*

### Post status updates from anywhere in iOS 6

One of the best features of iOS 6's Facebook integration is the ability to post a new status update from Notification Center, Safari and a whole host of other apps. To get set up, head into the Notifications tab and ensure the Share Widget and Facebook (if you'd like Wall posts, event invitations, etc. delivered as Notification banners) are both enabled in Notification Center, in the Settings tab.

To post a status update from Notification Center, swipe down from the top of your iPad's screen from anywhere in iOS, then tap the Tap

to Post button. A Share Sheet will appear on screen with a text field to type your Facebook status update. You can also add a location to your status and choose its privacy level by tapping on the relevant icons (Fig 2).

This isn't the only place you can post from. Links or photos can be posted from all over iOS 6. Simply head into the Photos app, select an image and tap the Share icon in the top corner. From here, tap the Facebook icon and you'll be presented with a Share Sheet, this time with the photo attached (Fig 3). This works for other apps, such as Safari, too, so it's worth exploring to see what you can share.

*Fig 1: You can choose which apps have access to Facebook integration in iOS 6 from the Settings app*

# "Whenever someone updates their phone number, it's instantly updated in Contacts"

## Sync your Calendars and Contacts

Like it or not, Facebook holds a lot of information about your life. While a lot of this information can be a little useless, some of it (such as email addresses and phone numbers) can be put to good use. iOS 6 and Facebook can sync so that email addresses, telephone numbers, etc. can be synced with the contacts on your iPad. That way whenever someone updates their email address or phone number, it's instantly updated in Contacts. To set this, just head to the Facebook tab in the Settings app and ensure that the on/off toggle next to Contacts is set to On (Fig 1).

If, for whatever reason, you don't want your contacts' numbers and email addresses synced with those on Facebook, then you can always grab their profile pictures (Fig 2) and nothing else, just tap on the Update All Contacts button.

Contacts isn't the only app Facebook can integrate with, either. Calendar can also show every Facebook event you've signed up to as part of its display of events, handy for ensuring you never miss that surprise party or all important gig (Fig 3). Again, this is as simple as ensuring Calendar access is switched on under the Facebook tab in Settings.

*Fig 2: Contact details, such as email address and phone number, are automatically updated for any of your friends on Facebook*

*Fig 3: Facebook events in your Calendar are marked with Facebook's logo for easy identification among everything else*

## Facebook sync
### Setting up Facebook integration in iOS 6

### 1: Hand over the details
Head into Settings. Under the Facebook tab, enter your login details.

### 2: Allow your apps access
Tap the toggle switches below to allow apps access to your account details.

### 3: Install the official app
Download the official app from the App Store to get maximum integration.

### 4: Set up your notifications
Head into Notifications in Settings and ensure the share widget is enabled.

# Twitter

Make the most of the additional Twitter integration in iOS 6 to share photos, websites and more with your friends and family using a few simple steps

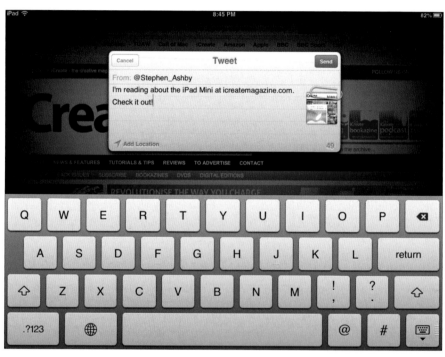

## Use it to:

- **Tweet photos fast**
  Quickly share photos through Twitter using the share button.

- **Share your favourite sites with friends**
  Tweet links to other websites from within Safari.

- **Get notifications automatically**
  Set up Notification Center to receive Twitter updates.

- **Import contact photos**
  Add Twitter avatars to all your contacts.

- **Contact your friends through Twitter**
  Use Contact sync to easily tweet your friends.

*Fig 1 (top left): The keyboard has been adapted to make tweeting easy, with the # and @ buttons*

*Fig 2 (bottom left): The Sharing button is available in all kinds of apps, thanks to Apple*

*Fig 3 (main image): Sharing Sheets make tweeting fast and simple.*

# Integrate Twitter with your iPad

## Log in to Twitter in iOS and use your iPad to send tweets

### Tweet from anywhere

One of the best things about the Twitter integration in iOS 6 is that it allows you to use the service no matter what you're doing. Whether you're browsing the web, watching a video or have simply taking a photo that you just want to share, you can do it with just a couple of taps.

All you need to do is look for the Sharing button that is present in many of Apple's own built-in apps. Tap it and you'll see a selection of sharing options, including Twitter. If you choose it, a Sharing Sheet will appear. Simply start typing to write your message; the

keyboard is adapted specifically for Twitter, so the hashtag (#) and at (@) buttons are both available with no extra taps required.

All of this is perfect for quickly tweeting a photo or video, but it can also be used in Safari to send a link; the App Store to share your favourite download; or even the Maps app to tweet a location. But the most brilliant part is the fact that Apple has released the tools that developers need to integrate the Sharing button into their own apps. So whether you're using an app that was built into iOS 6, or just one of your favourites from the App Store, sharing is simple via Twitter.

## Set up integration
Get all the benefits of
Twitter integration in iOS 6

### 1: Log in
Open Settings and scroll down to
Twitter in the left-hand bar, then log in.

### 2: Add more accounts
Tap the Add Account button and do the
same for all your other accounts.

### 3: Install the app
Tap the Install button at the top to install
the Twitter app, if you haven't already.

### 4: Limit apps
Use the sliders below to control multiple
apps that access Twitter.

*Fig 1: Adding your account in iOS 6 will only take a few minutes, but it offers more than just a fast tweeting experience*

# "Twitter scans the people you follow and adds their username to your Contact Card"

## Information and apps

For many, Twitter integration will be all about fast tweeting from whichever app their using, but this isn't the only use for the system in iOS 6. Setting up your account in the Settings panel (Fig. 1) will also offer the ability to download information from Twitter to your contacts. If, for example, you have the email addresses or full names of certain people in your Contacts app, Twitter will scan the people you follow, and your followers, and add their username to their Contact Card. This system additionally lets you add photos to all of your contacts for easy access.

The result is a much broader set of information for your friends, and it will also ensure that when tweeting from other apps, such as Photos, you can @ mention your friends by simply hitting the @ button and starting to type. iOS 6 will immediately start searching your contacts, so that you can instantly tap the name of the contact you were thinking of and see them tagged.

In addition, signing in to Twitter in Settings will offer other apps the ability to access your account for tweeting purposes. This can all be controlled easily, but for Twitter support system-wide it's a brilliant addition (Fig 3).

*Fig 2: You can update your contacts and see their twitter names and avatars downloaded onto your iPad*

*Fig 3: When you sign in, third party apps such as the brilliant Tweetbot can access your details for simple sign-in.*

# FaceTime

Apple's FaceTime app offers the perfect way to keep in touch with family and friends around the world with unique video chatting software for all your Apple devices

Fig 1 (far left): The Contacts tab allows you to view and edit all of your Contacts, without needing to open the dedicated app

Fig 2 (main image): During a call there is little on screen to distract you from the conversation you are having

Fig 3 (bottom left): You can add Favorites by tapping the '+' button in the top right of the app

## Use it to:

- **Chat with friends**
  Quickly talk with other Apple device users.

- **Use both cameras**
  Use the front-facing camera to show your face or the back to show your surroundings.

- **Get FaceTime on TV**
  Mirror your iPad's display on the big screen.

- **Manage contacts**
  View and edit contact information within the app.

- **View both ways**
  Rotate your device to either orientation to catch the whole picture.

# Chat face to face

## This little video-call app is a great way to keep in touch

### Navigating FaceTime

One reason why FaceTime is so much better than other video chat applications on the iPad is its simple user interface. During a call, the largest and clearest thing you will see is the person at the other end. In addition, buttons are kept to a minimum – just End and Mute – to avoid any distraction (Fig 2). There is also a small window in the corner of the screen that shows what the person on the other end of the call will see; this will be greyed out if you hit the Mute button, to show that the other user won't be able to hear what you're saying.

Outside of the call interface, things are still kept simple, with the primary focus being on the camera. Your face will take up most of the screen, with a bar on the right-hand side of it showing you Contacts (Fig 1), Recent calls or Favorites. You can add Favorites with a couple of taps, so you have quick and easy access to your most frequently called friends (Fig 3). In the Contacts tab you can view every contact on your iPad, find out when they last called you and even edit their data within the app, rather than having to head into the Contacts app to do so.

Fig 1: The Mac version offers HD call quality, so you will look fantastic to whoever you're speaking to

# "You can speak to any of your contacts, anywhere in the world, as long as they have any Apple device with a camera"

## Chat on multiple devices

While FaceTime, in its present form, may have started life as an iPhone and iPad app a couple of years ago, it was actually based on technology used in an app called iChat, which debuted on the Mac in 2002. The two apps weren't compatible, but last year Apple released a FaceTime app for their computers, which means that everyone can now enjoy video calling, no matter what Apple device they are currently using.

The Mac app looks and feels incredibly similar to that of the iPad and iPhone apps, as the interface is almost identical (Fig 1). However, thanks to the extra physical space available in Apple's laptops and desktop machines, there is extra room for the cameras, meaning that the newest machines have a FaceTime HD camera built in, offering up to 720p HD video quality for videos calls when the connected Wi-Fi network can handle it.

This means that you can speak to all of your friends and family as long as they have an iPhone, iPad (Figs 2 & 3) or any kind of Mac with a camera. While doing so, the live video you view will alays be incredibly crisp and clean. And, because the interface is so simple, everyone will find it easy to use, so even those who aren't familiar with computers will be available to you for a chat.

Fig 2 (far left): The iPad is a great way to talk with friends thanks to the large display and touch-screen interface

Fig 3 (left): You will get a smaller image on the iPhone, but it's still a great way of chatting on the go

## Switch cameras
You iPad has two cameras, so let's use them with FaceTime

### 1: Start a call
Choose who you want to talk to from your Contacts or Favorites list.

### 2: Flip it
At the bottom of the screen, tap the camera button with two arrows.

### 3: Flip back
To flip back to the front-facing camera, tap the button again.

### 4: End call
When you've finished, tap the End Call button at the bottom of the screen.

**Wi-Fi and 3G**
You'll have to be connected to a Wi-Fi or 3G network in order to make calls using FaceTime on your Apple device

**Search**
The Search bar at the top of the column will allow you to quickly find the person you want; it will self-update as you type

**Camera**
The camera is always on when you're using the FaceTime app – even when you're just browsing through contacts, you will see yourself on the screen

**Contacts**
You can access all of your contacts using the tab in the bottom-right corner of the screen, and add new ones from the top

## Manage contacts

There are some occasions when you'll be using FaceTime and just want to quickly add a new contact to your iPad. Rather than closing the app, open the Contacts app and add it there, before heading back into FaceTime. It's possible to quickly add contacts, or edit previously existing contacts within the FaceTime app itself.

This means that while you might have phone numbers and an address for a contact, you may not have their Apple ID on record. Without it, you won't be able to speak with them on FaceTime. If this is the case, it's possible to edit the contact by simply tapping the 'Edit' button in the top-right corner of the screen and adding the extra information. This screen also allows you to clean up your contacts by deleting those you no longer need, and gives you quick links if you'd rather send them a message, share the contact

with others, or add that person to your list of Favorites for faster access later.

There is also a Refresh button at the top of the contacts list. Add a new contact to another device which is set up with your iCloud account and you can instantly access it on your iPad by tapping here.

*Fig 1 (right): You can view individual contact cards to choose which address or number you wish to contact*

*Fig 2 (far right): Your contacts will be listed on the right of the screen and they can be searched quickly*

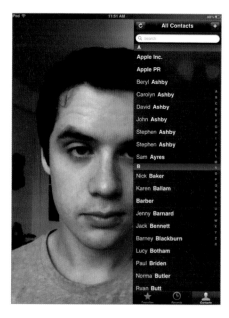

## Import contacts

The Contacts section of FaceTime is a quick and simple way to access the details of your friends so that you can keep up to date with them using video chat. Adding new contacts is extremely simply as just tapping the '+' in the top corner will give you a new card that can be filled in with as many or as few details as you want.

And, because everything in iOS is so neatly integrated, this contact will automatically be added to your Contacts app on the iPad, so if you need to view that card again, you don't

have to do it in FaceTime (Fig 2). This process also works the other way around, meaning you can add contacts in the Contacts app and have them instantly available in FaceTime.

And, of course, now that iCloud exists, it's even easier to share Contacts across a number of devices. If you have an iPhone, as well as an iPad, add a new contact to that device (Fig 3). iCloud will sync it immediately to your other devices, so that the next time you pick up your iPad, the contact has automatically been imported and is ready to use for a FaceTime call on your tablet.

## "Now that iCloud exists, it's easier to share Contacts across a number of devices"

*Fig 1 (left):*
*Make sure*
*iCloud is enabled*
*in your Settings*
*menu to sync*
*contacts from*
*other devices*

*Fig 2 (below left): With iCloud enabled, even contacts you add on other devices will be added to your FaceTime app*

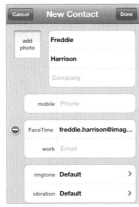

*Fig 3: Add contacts on your iPhone and they'll be imported into FaceTime on iPad*

## Use another app
You can use other apps while chatting in FaceTime

### 1: Start talking
Start a FaceTime call. If you need to check something during it, you can.

### 2: Go home
To start using another app, first you need to press the Home button.

### 3: Browsing
Choose the app you want to use and tap it to open it up. Browse it as normal.

### 4: Return
When you are finished, tap the green bar at the top to return to your call.

# FaceTime

## Mute a call
### Stop the people on the other end from hearing you

### 1: Switch it off
Tap the Mute button at the bottom of the screen. Your image should turn grey.

### 2: Switch it on
Tap the button again to switch your mic back on so your friend can hear you.

### 3: Volume
You can use the volume buttons on the side of the iPad to alter levels as normal.

### 4: Say goodbye
When you're ready to go, press the End button to hang up the call.

### See yourself
This box shows what your camera can see. You can move this around with your finger and pin it into corners

### Controls
The controls will sit at the bottom of the screen at all times – tapping won't get rid of them

## FaceTime on your TV
With the release of iOS 5 last year, it was announced that a new feature for the iPad, called AirPlay Mirroring, would enable users to view whatever was on their iPad (2 or later) screen to their TV as long as they had an Apple TV connected. The small box hooks up to your television set and connects to your local Wi-Fi network. On your iPad you can then activate AirPlay (Fig 1), switch on Mirroring and your screen should instantly appear on your TV. This is fantastic for some apps, like games and photo slideshow apps, but it also works brilliantly with FaceTime.

Sadly, as the system only mirrors what's on your iPad's screen, it's not possible to simply put your tablet down and speak directly at the TV. You will need to keep the iPad pointing at you so the camera is still on you, but if you want a room full of people to be able to speak to the person on the other end of the call (Fig 3), Mirroring your iPad onto your TV is a fantastic way of doing this. And, as it's all wireless, it's a seamless experience. There is also an accessory called the A/V Adaptor that allows you to simply wire up your iPad to an HDMI port on your TV for similar results.

*Fig 3: You can use FaceTime just as normal, but whatever appears on your screen will also appear on the TV*

*Fig 1 (right): In the multitasking bar, swipe right and open the AirPlay menu*

*Fig 2 (below): When connected, this blue bar will appear at the top and pulse*

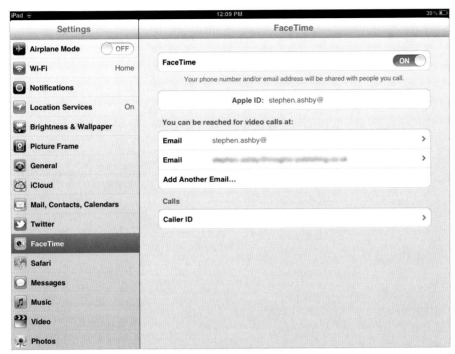

Fig 1: First of all, check that FaceTime is switched on in the appropriate section of the Settings menu

# "You need to be connected to Wi-Fi or 3G to make and receive FaceTime calls"

## Troubleshooting FaceTime

There could be several reasons why FaceTime isn't working for you. If you're having problems making or receiving calls, go to the Settings app. Choose FaceTime from the list on the left and check that the service is turned on with the switch at the top of the page (Fig 1). Flicking this off and on again may fix some issues. It's also important to note that you will need to be connected to Wi-Fi or a 3G network to make and receive FaceTime calls. The 3G update came with iOS 6.

If you can't even see the FaceTime app on your iPad, it may have been disabled in Restrictions (Fig 2). Open up the Settings app and choose General, then Restrictions. In here is a list of apps that can be restricted on your iPad. Check that FaceTime and Camera are both set to On – if they aren't, the feature simply won't be available.

You may also be experiencing problems if the date and time of your device is incorrect. To fix this, open Settings and tap General, then Date & Time (Fig 3). Flick the button next to Set Automatically to the On position to make sure the time is correct. If all else fails and you still can't connect with FaceTime, switch your iPad off and on again.

Fig 2: If the FaceTime icon isn't appearing on your Home screen, check the Restrictions section and switch it on

Fig 3: The Time & Date settings may be causing problems – open them up from the Settings menu and choose Set Automatically

## Add another address
People can reach you using more than one email address

### 1: Settings
Open the Settings app and tap FaceTime from the options on the left.

### 2: New address
Tap 'Add Another Email…' at the bottom of the list.

### 3: Type and verify
Type in the address and press Return so the iPad verifies it.

### 4: Caller ID
Tap Caller ID at the bottom to change it to your new address.

# Siri

Apple's native personal assistant responds to your voice commands, takes down your dictations, publishes posts to your social network and provides handy, invaluable and current information

*Fig 1 (above): When your search results are displayed, Siri will automatically open Safari so you can see all the answers on offer*

*Fig 2 (top left): You can Siri anything and it will turn it into a web search, showing you the results in just a few seconds*

*Fig 3 (main image): Siri will use the native interface of certain apps where applicable when it shows you certain search results*

## Use it to:

- **Send messages**
  Tell Siri to send a text to a friend, and it does as told

- **Check the weather**
  Siri will give you up-to-date weather information

- **Find a restaurant**
  Ask for a pizza place nearby and Siri will list them for you

- **Check the score**
  Latest scores, fixture and league standings on your favourite soccer team

- **Stay social**
  Twitter is integrated into iOS so you can ask Siri to send tweets on behalf of you

- **Launch an app**
  Simply say 'Play Angry Birds' to launch the app

# Your personal assistant

## Use your voice for a completely hands-free experience

### Search the web

The beauty of Siri is that as it is fully integrated into most aspects of iOS, so you can use it to search and discover almost anything. It can access all of your apps as well as native programmes, including Safari. All you have to do is ask it for something, and Siri will go to the relevant place and return with the relevant information that you requested. For example, if you wanted to know the weather, Siri's results would use the native weather app that draws its information from the web. Siri even takes aspects of the app's interface to show it's results, as you can see in Fig 2.

Where the information you're looking for can't be accessed from an app, Siri uses your words as the basis of a web search, transferring you to Safari and instantly showing you the result. You can also specifically request a web search by starting your instruction with 'search the web for'. Siri will then perform a Google search and display the result for you. These results are shown to you full screen as opposed to in the standard Siri window so if need be you can jump in and get more involved in the outcome of the search process. This is effortless web searching, where you don't even have to lift a finger.

Fig 1: The information guide shows you the full extent of what Siri can do in terms of using Siri to find and reach locations

# "Siri is very helpful when it comes to finding places nearby with their ratings"

## Get directions and find places around you

Being integrated in iOS means that Siri has complete access to Apple Maps, and can therefore be used to find you directions between any two places, as well as from your current location to a more familiar one. To get a clearer idea of just how you can put Siri and Maps to good use, open the Siri window and tap the information icon next to the welcome message. Here you can see all the different things you can ask Siri, one of which is focussed around directions. Tap this option to see a full list of the ways you can use Siri

to reach, as well as find locations, businesses and points of interest. Once you have an idea of the sort of scope on offer, you can begin to use Siri to guide you from place to place.

The other main area that Siri is very helpful is when it comes to finding places nearby. Using your location, Siri will create a list of Indian restaurants, for example (Fig 3), and place them in order of rating – with scores coming by way of Yelp. You can then tap any of the names on the list to see those reviews, more information and their location plotted on the map. All you have to do now is pick up the phone and make a booking.

Fig 2: You can ask for directions to anywhere, and Siri will quickly produce a route plotted on your iPad map

Fig 3: When it comes to finding places, Siri will create a list for you, arranged by location and rating, with more details available in a tap

## Change the settings
### Alter Siri's settings to best suit your preferences

### 1: Settings
In order to make changes to Siri, you need to head to the Settings app.

### 2: Find Siri
There is a dedicated Siri section, which can be found under the General tab.

### 3: Silence the Voice
Turn off Siri by tapping the switch and confirming via the pop-up message.

### 4: Language
To change Siri's language, tap Language and select from the list.

**App Interfaces**

Where applicable, Siri will use its own version of app interfaces to show you things like weather forecasts and stock prices

**Adjust**

You can adjust anything you ask Siri by tapping on your command and using the keyboard to type it out as you wish

**Speak**

You can tap the Siri icon at any point to ask a new question or give a new command to the app

**History**

You can look back through any single Siri session by scrolling up, should you forget something you asked earlier

## Find what you're looking for

Apple's website proclaims that your wish is Siri's command, and the range of wishes that can be fulfilled is pretty impressive. Ask Siri for the score from yesterday's game and you get it, with a dedicated score board for each sport and a scoring breakdown. You can also ask Siri for league standings to see how your team are getting on in the grand scheme of things.

Of course sport might not be your thing, so you can use Siri to help you find a movie to go see. Not only that, but you can use Siri to find a time and a cinema. You can even watch the

trailer with a tap of the movie poster as well as read reviews and search by certain actors, actress', producers or director.

Even if what you're looking for is within your phone, Siri can make it easier to find. As part of the iOS 6 update, it is now possible to open an app just by asking Siri to do so. Start your command with 'Open' or 'Play' and Siri will take you right to it. The same is true when it comes to your reminders and schedule, so when you're on the way to work you can ask Siri to show you your appointments for the day, and plan your time around them.

## "Ask Siri for the score from yesterday's game, or the weather in another location, and you will get it"

Fig 1: If you missed the game last night, you can just ask Siri to show you how your team faired

Fig 2: As well as scores, Siri can now show you standings and statistics across a range of sports

Fig 3: Siri allows you to search for movies and cinemas near you, and then watch the trailer before finding a screening time

Fig 1: You can dictate almost anything to Siri, and that includes your latest social network update

# "'Write on my wall' is all you need to say to Siri to update your Facebook status"

## Dictate using Siri

The power of your voice when combined with Siri is a great productivity tool, and if you're in a position where you can't type on your iPad, you can dictate to Siri to send all manner of communications. This ranges from the more light-hearted of posts - for example you can ask Siri to tweet for you - all the way up to dictating important emails and sending them. To post to a social network like Facebook or Twitter, all you have to do is specify in your command stating clearly what you would like to do. 'Write on my wall' is all you need

to say for Facebook. Simply asking Siri to tweet something also works thanks to the integration of Twitter and Facebook into iOS.

If you want to quickly make a note of something before you forget, just ask Siri to note it and it will be added to the native app of the same name. Ask Siri to send an email and it will come back at you asking for contacts, a subject and the message itself. Of course, you don't even have to be on the home screen to dictate to Siri, there's a handy dictate button built into the keyboard, which you can use at any point.

Fig 2: Quickly make a note of something by asking Siri to jot it down for you

Fig 3: Ask Siri to send an email and it will take down all the important details and send it for you

## Send an email
Complete all your important correspondence hands-free

### 1: Prompt
Simply ask Siri to send an email, or to respond to one you already have.

### 2: Contact
Once you have the email open, Siri will ask you who you would like to send it to.

### 3: Subject
Next up is the subject bar, with Siri again asking you for the details.

### 4: The Text
Finally, dictate the content of the email and Siri will check it before sending.

# Camera

The iPad camera can be useful on many occasions and for so many tasks. There are a lot of useful features built in. It's time to understand them

Fig 1 (above): You can take good photos with the iPad if you take your time and keep things steady

Fig 2 (top left): The grid option will help you to keep your images straight when you capture them

Fig 3 (main image): Simply tap the capture button on the right to quickly take a photo of whatever the iPad camera is viewing

## Use it to:

- **Take great photos**
  You can take some very impressive photos using the iPad camera.

- **Utilise FaceTime**
  The front and back cameras work well with FaceTime.

- **Edit perfectly**
  Photos can be edited to make them just right.

- **Capture video**
  You can capture videos when the moments arise.

- **Shoot self-portraits**
  Just tap a button to take a self-portrait.

# Take photos anywhere

Use your iPad to capture photos of anything, any time you like

### Shoot photos

The iPad is not exactly a natural picture-taker because of the device's size, but its camera works extremely well in a variety of situations. Simply tap the Camera icon in the Home screen and a view of whatever the iPad's rear lens is looking at will pop up. You can then tap the capture icon on the right to quickly snap a photo (see Fig 3). At the bottom you will see an 'Options' button. When you tap this you will see a Grid on/off icon pop up. Tap it to place a grid over the camera screen (which you can see in Fig 1). This is useful for

ensuring that your photos are kept as straight as possible and will save you time having to tweak them afterwards.

If you take your time and ensure that you are holding the iPad steady, you should be able to capture photos at a quality that looks as good as a decent smartphone, and so there is no reason to ignore the iPad camera any more – especially if you have a new iPad. No matter how you hold the iPad, the capture button will always be on the right and will quickly feel very natural to use despite the relatively large size of the iPad itself.

*Fig 1: The slider at the bottom right of the screen is what you use to start capturing videos*

# "The new iPad has image stabilisation built in and can also take 1080p HD video"

## Shoot videos

Capturing video on the iPad may seem like an even stranger thing to do than taking photos, but it actually works very well thanks to the larger screen. You really can see what is happening in front of you and capture events as you see them. At the bottom-right of the Camera screen, you will see a slider (see Fig 1). When you tap this, it will automatically change the capture mechanism to video and you can start capturing footage straight away.

Once you have tapped the slider, a new icon will appear on screen which indicates which mode the iPad is in. Tap it and you will

start shooting a video – a timer will also pop up on screen showing how much video you have taken so far (Fig 2). If you're shooting with an iPad 2, you will need to be careful not to move it around too much because it is very easy to lose focus and videos can quickly become blurred at important moments. You can see this effect in the third image (Fig 3).

However, the good news is that the new iPad has image stabilisation built in and is also capable of taking 1080p HD video, which pits it very competitively against more professional cameras for quality.

*Fig 2: Simply tap the circular icon to start capturing video straight away. The timer shows how much you have taken*

*Fig 3: Videos can become blurred if you move the iPad around too much when capturing content*

## Time to FaceTime
Use the front and rear cameras to great effect

### 1: Camera flip icon
At the bottom of the screen is an icon with a camera in it and two arrows.

### 2: Front camera view
Tap the icon and you will see a moving image of yourself on screen.

### 3: Video chat also available
Go to Settings>FaceTime and enter your Apple ID to start video conversations.

### 4: Chat for free at any time
Choose a contact and hit FaceTime to call them for free, using both cameras.

**Snap a picture**
Use the icon on the right-hand side to quickly snap a photo or take a video whenever the moment arises

**Videos and photos**
A simple swipe of the slider will swap you between photo and video capture mode in a second

**The grid**
The grid function is particularly useful for ensuring that all of your photos are as straight as possible at all times

**Two cameras**
You can also quickly swap between the front and rear cameras, which is useful for video chatting through FaceTime

Grid ON
Done

## Video editing and trimming

Once you have captured a video, it is highly likely that it won't be the exact length you require. Open the Camera Roll and select a video you have taken. Notice the frame strip at the top of the screen (see Fig 1). Use your left thumb and drag the left-side band along the frame strip. You can move it to any position and the strip will expand to allow extremely accurate positioning (Fig 2).

Once you've found your start position you can use your right thumb to move the right-side band to the position that you want the video to finish at (see Fig 3). A 'Trim' icon will pop up and tapping this will cut the video down to the exact size and length you require.

The process can take 2 seconds or 10 minutes depending on how precise you want to be, but taking time with this feature can greatly improve any video you take. Sometimes what you leave out is as important as what is included. If you want to take your editing further, search for 'iMovie' in the App Store and check out our guide to it later in the book.

Fig 1: The frame strip at the top lets you trim any iPad video you have taken

Fig 2: You can go to any location in the video and be extremely precise thanks to the visual indicators

Fig 3: Tap the 'Trim' icon to cut down the video to the exact length you require and to remove the boring bits

Fig 1: Add the Camera app to the dock for much quicker access when in a hurry

Fig 2: The volume button is a quick way to take a photo, but it is close to the lens – so be careful!

# "Another trick is to use the volume-up button when taking photos"

## Take faster photos

The standard procedure to take a photograph on an iPad is not as quick as it could be. Besides the obvious logistical problems of picking it up and then going through the process of unlocking it etc, there is an easier way to take photos which should help you achieve better quality and to take them much quicker.

Highlight the camera icon on the Home screen and hold it down, and then drag it to the dock (as shown in Fig 1 above). This means that when you unlock the iPad, you can jump straight to the camera. Another trick is to use the volume-up button when taking photos. It works exactly the same way as the capture icon on the screen, but means you can hold the iPad steady. It is close to the lens, however, so be careful not to place your finger in the wrong position (as we managed to do several times!).

Another way to ensure faster photo capture is to keep the Camera app held in an open state. You can check by double-tapping the Home button and this will ensure that the app does not need time to start up.

## Share your videos
### Get your masterpieces published online

### 1: Shoot and edit
Capture your video and edit it to perfection as normal.

### 2: Share arrow
Tap the share arrow to reveal a menu with four sharing options.

### 3: Message
'Message' will attach your video to an iMessage that you can send.

### 4: Send to YouTube
'Send to YouTube' will share your video to the popular website (account needed).

# Camera

## Use grid lines to compose
### Getting things straight

### 1: Difficult to straighten up
It is often difficult to see straight when looking at an object through a screen.

### 2: Find the grid
Tap the 'Options' button, then move the slider to 'On' to bring up the grid.

### 3: Find the right lines
You can now easily line up straight parts of an object with a grid line.

### 4: The centre of a photo
To make an object fill a certain amount of the photo, fit it in the grid squares.

**View the zoom slider**
Place your finger and thumb on the screen and the slider will pop up for you to manipulate as you see fit

**Time to zoom**
Slide your finger along the slider and you will see the image zoom in and out. It's very easy to use

## iPad camera controls
Focus is especially important when taking any photo – whether you're taking it on an iPad 2 or DSLR camera – but you may often want to focus on a specific area that is not in the centre of the scene. As you can see in Fig 1, we have tapped the area of the screen where a box has popped up. This specific area will be the main focus of the image and this simple feature enables you to focus on any area you like.

The touch focusing feature does, however, work much better on shots where objects are further away (Fig 2) and you need to experiment a little to find the type of focusing that works best for you. With any iPad camera shot, you also need to remember that good lighting is often needed to get clarity in the parts you want.

You can also zoom by simply pinching with your fingers. This is a very simple and effective feature, but remember that zooming in too far will almost certainly result in a photo that is too blurry to be usable in any way. The zooming feature is slightly too ambitious for the lens at times, so be aware of the maximum level you should push it to so that the resulting photos are worth using.

*Fig 1: Simply tap the screen to focus on a specific part of the view you are looking at*

*Fig 2: You will find that the touch focusing works better on longer-distance shots*

*Fig 1: In landscape mode, the controls will be set as you would expect to see them*

## Shooting landscapes and portraits

Taking photos and videos in different orientations is very easy on an iPad, but consideration should be given to how the controls work. When you change the orientation of the iPad, the capture button will jump to the right and the other controls move accordingly. In Fig 1, the capture button is where it should be and a landscape picture seems to suit the subject matter better.

In Fig 2, the controls have moved, but a portrait shot is not necessarily the best orientation for this type of shot. Take some time to consider the best way and don't always choose the same method – it's the subject matter that should lead you to decide which is best. One other point to remember is that landscape is the default orientation for iPad picture and video taking and so space will be lost either side in portrait mode, as you can see in Figure 3. You can lock the orientation by either going to Settings>General and choosing 'Lock Rotation' or by double-tapping the Home button and sliding the dock to the right. Here you will see an icon that lets you lock the screen in whatever position it is currently residing. Locking the orientation can greatly help improve the quality and overall look of your iPad photos.

*Fig 2: The controls jump when the iPad is switched to portrait mode, to keep the familiar interface intact*

*Fig 3: Portrait mode is not the default on an iPad and therefore some space will be wasted either side*

## Access the Camera Roll in different ways
### Find the Camera Roll

### 1: Access via the icon
The icon at the bottom left gives you immediate access to the Camera Roll.

### 2: Swipe to see last photo
In the Camera app, swipe to the right to see the last photo or video you took.

### 3: From the lock screen
Tap the picture icon on the lock screen to see photos set in Settings>Picture Frame.

### 4: Access from apps
Many apps let you access the Camera Roll for images to use or manipulate.

# Photos

Photos might seem like a fairly unexciting app, but this rather unassuming icon on your iPad's home screen hides some incredibly powerful image management and editing tools

## Use it to:

- **View and share photos**
  View and share photos with friends via Photo Stream.

- **Edit images**
  Enhance your images.

- **Create a slideshow**
  View your pictures in style, with the option of AirPlay.

- **Use Photo Stream**
  Stream and share your pics from iCloud with ease.

- **Sync images**
  Sync your photos to and from your computer.

- **Create video**
  Play, stream and organise video footage.

- **Print pictures**
  Print one or multiple shots with AirPrint.

*Fig 1 (top left): A full suite of thumbnails provides you with a quick and easy method to view your photo album*

*Fig 2 (main image): Photos can be stored in your iPad for later use and manipulation*

*Fig 3 (bottom left): The pinch gesture command can be used to zoom in to any image*

# Manage your photographs

## Use your iPad to manipulate and control your picture collection

### The Camera Roll

Apple's built-in Photos app lets you view photos and videos that you capture or sync to your iPad in your Camera Roll album in the Photos app. Photos and videos that you take with the built-in camera or save from an email, text message, webpage or screenshot are all included here.

Tap on the album to see its full suite of thumbnails (Fig 1). Then you can tap a thumbnail image to see the photo itself or a video played at full-screen (Fig 2).

Use the pinch gesture command to return to thumbnail view or to close an album.

Likewise, you can use the expand gesture to open an album, zoom into a photo or view a video in full-screen (Fig 3).

There are a number of associated commands within this area, such as showing or hiding the controls and scrollbar at the bottom by tapping the full-screen photo or video, flicking the screen left or right to see the next or previous photo or video, using a double-tapping or pinching gesture to zoom in or out of the screen, dragging the photo to pan it around the screen, tapping the centre of a video to play it, or using AirPlay to stream a photo to an HDTV.

*Fig 1: Once Photo Stream has been turned on, it will save images to your iCloud*

# "You can select multiple images and create a shared Photo Stream album"

## Photo Stream

With Photo Stream, your photos are automatically uploaded to iCloud and then synced to the rest of your Photo Stream-enabled, such as your iPhone or Mac.

To turn on Photo Stream, go to Settings> iCloud>Photo Stream. New photos that you have taken are uploaded to your Photo Stream, when the iPad is connected to the internet via Wi-Fi (Fig 1). Any other photos added to your Camera Roll are also uploaded to your Photo Stream collection and then pushed to your other devices. Photo Stream can store up to 1,000 of your most recent photos across all your iOS devices.

To save photos to your iPad's internal storage from Photo Stream, go to the Photo Stream album, click the sharing icon (top right), select the photos that you wish to save and then select the save destination (Fig 2). To delete a photo from iCloud, go to the Photo Stream album, select photo and then tap the Trash icon in the top right and confirm (Fig 3).

In iOS 6, you can select multiple images from your Photo stream and create a shared Photo Stream album with family and friends. Check out the sidebar on the right to find out how to set these up.

*Fig 2: You can save your photos to a variety of destinations, from your iPad*

*Fig 3: A series of photos can all be highlighted and deleted at the same time*

## Share Photo Stream
Share snaps with family and friends via iCloud

### 1: Select your snaps
In Photo Stream, tap the Edit button and select the photos you'd like to share.

### 2: Find the option
Now tap the Share button and, from the options available, tap Photo Stream.

### 3: Find some friends
Enter the details of those you'd like to share your photos with.

### 4: Comment and post
Add a comment to your shared Photo Stream album then tap Post to finish.

# Photos

**Select a view**
Tapping on any of the options in the top bar will choose which way your photos are displayed

**Slideshow**
Tapping this button will bring a set of slideshow options so you can show off your photos and images in style

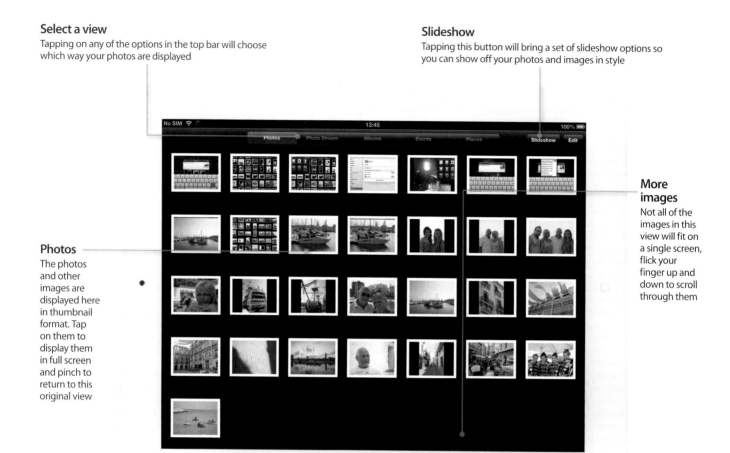

**Photos**
The photos and other images are displayed here in thumbnail format. Tap on them to display them in full screen and pinch to return to this original view

**More images**
Not all of the images in this view will fit on a single screen, flick your finger up and down to scroll through them

## Edit your photos

Using your iPad to take photos is quick and easy, but there is much more you can do with the handy Photos app apart from storing your images. Use it to quickly edit your images as soon as you take them. There are a range of easy methods to edit your iPad photos.

There are four basic edits you can perform using the Photos app. While viewing a photo in its full-screen format, tap the Edit button

and then choose one of the four available tools: they are Rotate, Enhance, Red-Eye and Crop. Rotate allows you to change the physical alignment of the images by rotating it at different 90 degree angles (Fig 2). Enhance improves the overall look and feel of the image. It works by improving the photo's overall darkness or lightness, colour saturation and other qualities. The Red-eye option (see page 115) is perfect for easily correcting red

eye - a result of flash light reflecting off the back of the subject's retina. After you've clicked the Red-Eye option, just tap the subject's eye for instant correction. The Crop Auto option helps you to tidy an image by erasing unwanted items surrounding that image. This helps you focus on the central image by removing excess clutter (Fig 3). To crop a picture, drag the corners of the grid to the required position and drag the photo to reposition.

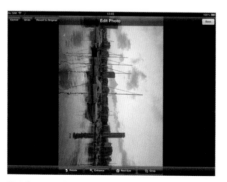
*Fig 1: When you click on the Edit button, a range of editing options appears at the base of the screen*

*Fig 2: If you aren't happy with your photo's orientation, press the Rotate button to change it*

*Fig 3: When you want to crop a photograph, a grid pattern sits on top of your image to allow adjustment*

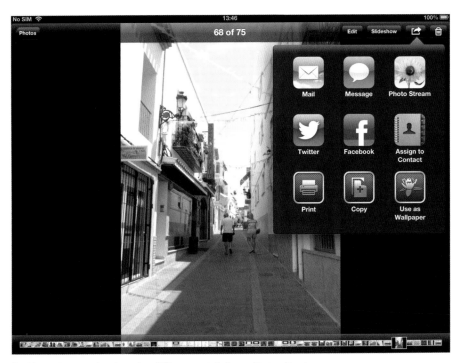

Fig 1: You can share your photos in a variety of different ways including email, text and tweet

# "You can send photos via email, iMessage, Facebook, or Twitter"

## Share your shots with ease

Sharing your photos is simple. You can do this via email, iMessage, Facebook or Twitter. To get started, choose a photo from the thumbnail and tap it. If you don't see the Share icon shown in the image above, tap the screen to show the controls (Fig 1). Before you post an image to either of the social networks integrated with iOS 6, you must be logged into that relevant account. To do this, go to Settings and log in under the Twitter or Facebook tabs (Fig 2).

To send multiple photos, tap Edit while viewing your photo thumbnails, select the photos you want and then tap Share. You can also copy a photo by touching and holding it and then selecting Copy.

You also have the option to paste a photo (or video) in an email or text message to send (Fig 3). Touch and hold where you want to place it, then tap Paste. Alternatively, you can save a photo from an email message. Just tap to download, tap the photo, then tap Save.

To save a photo or video from a text message, tap the image in the conversation, then tap Save. Finally, to save a photo from a webpage, touch and hold the photo, then tap Save Image.

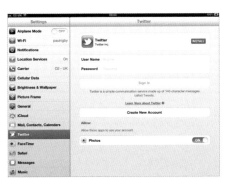

Fig 2: Before you tweet your photos, go to Settings to set up your Twitter account ready for tweeting

Fig 3: If you decide to share your photo within an email, your iPad will automatically place your photo into the message

## Share via Facebook

Post your best photos to everyone's favourite website

### 1: Connect to Facebook
If you haven't already, open the Setting app and login under the Facebook tab.

### 2: Select and share
In the Photos app, select an image then tap the Share icon in the top right and select the Facebook icon.

### 3: No comment?
It's entirely optional, but you can add a comment to go with your photo by typing it into the Share Sheet on screen.

### 4: Where are you?
Before hitting Post, add your location by tapping Add Location in the corner.

# Open images in style
Pinch to expand and rotate your photos and albums

## 1: Open albums
To find your photo albums, open Photos then tap the Albums button at the top.

## 2: Scroll for target stack
Locate your stack of choice by scrolling through your collection.

## 3: Pinch to open
Place your thumb and first finger on a stack, then push apart to open it.

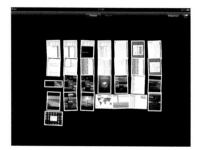

## 4: Pinch photos
You can also pinch and rotate your photos to create cool effects.

### Albums
When you enter this screen, the thumbnail images have an obvious 'stacked' quality to differentiate them from a photo thumbnail

### Rearrange
To rearrange a stack, tap the Edit button then drag any of the wiggling stacks to a new position on the screen

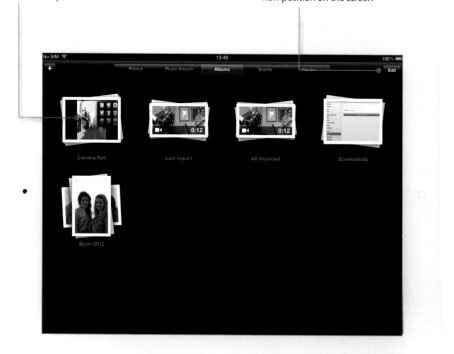

## Slideshows
To view a slideshow, enter the Photos app then tap on the Slideshows button on the top right of the screen. Tap once to drop a menu down that features two options. The first is a Transitions button that includes a dissolve, cube, ripple, wipe or origami dissolve (Fig 1). You also get the option of playing music while the slideshow is under way. If you turn the music option on, a new option appears that lists those music pieces sitting in your songs directory (Fig 2). From here, you can choose which piece of music to utilise.

There are further options available in the Settings app. Open that up and tap on the Photos button. Here, you can decide how long each image should stay on the screen: from 2 to 20 seconds per frame. You can also decide to repeat the entire slideshow sequence over and over or you can agree to undertake the slideshow but 'shuffle' the order of the images.

To stop the slideshow, tap the screen once to freeze it on the currently displayed photo. You also have the option to stream a slideshow to an HDTV using AirPlay. Start the video, slideshow or music, then enter the multitasking bar, swipe left to find the up arrow and choose the AirPlay device. Once streaming starts, you can exit the app that's playing the content.

*Fig 1: One of the options is to choose the type of transition effect used between shots in your slideshow*

*Fig 2: Click on the Slideshow button to reveal transitions and music options for the feature*

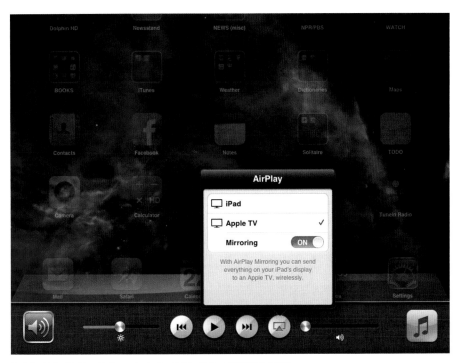

Fig 1: Double tap the Home button and swipe from left to right to access AirPlay options

# "You can mirror the iPad screen on a television with Apple TV"

## AirPlay and AirPrint

There are a number of methods to transfer photo files to other devices via a range of services. One of those is streaming data via a wireless network. It is possible, for example, to stream photos wirelessly to your HDTV using AirPlay and Apple TV. Both your iPad and the AirPlay-enabled device must be set up on the same Wi-Fi network.

Display the photo or a related slideshow, then tap and choose the AirPlay device. To access the AirPlay controls, when the iPad screen is on, double-click the Home button. You will see the slim multitasking bar appear

at the bottom of the screen. Press your finger on the bar and scroll to the left (Fig 1). Look out for the up-arrow button to switch on the AirPlay feature. To return to the iPad, tap the up arrow and choose iPad (Fig 2).

You can mirror the iPad screen on a television with Apple TV: everything on the iPad screen appears on the TV. Tap at the left end of the multitasking bar, choose an Apple TV and tap the Mirroring button that appears. You can also take advantage of AirPrint to get a physical copy of your best images. Hit the Share arrow and then Print (Fig 3). You must, however, have an AirPrint-ready printer.

Fig 2: Return to the iPad by clicking on the up arrow and then selecting the iPad option

Fig 3: Tap the Share arrow and then hit Print to print from an AirPrint-compatible printer

## Create a new album
Organise your photos with the intuitive album system

### 1: View your photos
In Photos, view the images and press the Share icon in the top right.

### 2: Select your albums
Tap to select the photos you want to add to the new album.

### 3: Add to an album
Click the Add To… button, which will bring up the Add To New Album option.

### 4: Name your album
Click the Add To New Album option, then type in a new album name.

# Photos

## Rearrange albums
### Change the order of the albums

### 1: Enter Photos app
To start rearranging your albums, enter the Photos app.

### 2: Select the Albums tab
Move to the top of the screen and select the Albums tab.

### 3: Free the stack
Press the selected album to rearrange. The stack of photos will free itself from the background.

### 4: Drag the stack
Drag the stack to the new location and release to drop it in that position.

### Select photos in Photo Stream
You can delete your photos from the Photo Stream collection. Firstly select the photos that you would like to delete

### Delete photos in Photo Stream
Once you have selected the photos you want to delete, press the red Delete button at the top left

## Places
If you have geotagged your photos – by shooting them with a GPS-enabled camera, for example – then your pictures will appear in the Places area based on their geographic co-ordinates. Within the Photos app - at the top of the general photos screen - select the Places tab. This will transfer the view to a world map. Your photos will be tagged with a red pin to indicated the location where they were taken (Fig 1). To explore the location, click on a red pin to see what images have been associated with the pin at that particular location. A miniature thumbnail image will appear over the head of the pin. If more than one image has been clicked at that location, the photos will be stacked into an album (Fig 2). You can view all of the photos connected to a particular geotag by tapping on the album. This takes you to an album view with all of the photos arranged in rows, from where each photo can then be viewed and edited individually. To view another photo or geotagged album, tap on a new red pin and a new thumbnail will appear on the screen. Use the gesture movement to zoom into the map. This will give you a more accurate view of the red pins and where the images were taken.

Fig 1: If you have geotagged your photographs then they will appear on the map, ready for inspection

Fig 2: Tap on a pin to reveal the images that have been associated with that location

Fig 1: Once connected, the iPad software will tell you what photo files are available for import from your connected device

# "Using the Camera Connection Kit, you can import photos from a digital camera"

## Import with the Camera Connection Kit

Using the iPad's Camera Connection Kit, you can import photos directly from a digital camera or an SD memory card. To connect a camera, make sure the camera is turned on, is in transfer mode and connect it to the camera connection kit using a USB cable (usually supplied with the camera itself). To use an SD memory card, insert the card into the slot on the SD Card Reader. This process also works with a Lightning or Dock connector and another iOS device. Once you've hooked everything up, the Photos app will open and display the photos that are available for

importing. Select the photos and videos that you want to import or tap Import All. To import just some of the items, tap the images that you want to include (a tick appears on each), tap Import, then select Import Selected. After the photos have been imported, keep or delete the photos and videos on the card, camera or iOS device. Then you can remove the SD Card Reader or the Camera Connector. To later examine the images, look in the last album that you have imported. To transfer the photos to your computer, connect the iPad using its dock connector and use iTunes or another application like iPhoto to copy your images over. It's that easy.

Fig 2: The Camera Connection Kit includes two connectors: one to connect a camera, the other to read an SD card

Fig 3: You can connect with USB and use iPhoto to import, but the Camera Connection Kit cuts out the middle man

## Get rid of red-eye
Improve the look of your portraits by removing red-eye

### 1: Select your photo
Open up the Photos app and select the offending image from your Camera Roll.

### 2: Hit the Edit button
Tap on the Edit button to bring the Red-Eye option onto the screen.

### 3: Red-eye removal
Tap on each of the red eyes to remove the unwanted effect.

### 4: Apply and accept
Tap Apply to accept and finish off the editing process. Save your image.

# Photo Booth

Photo Booth is all about fun, and it takes very little time to create some great effects which will amuse and horrify in equal measure. We show you how to get started

Fig 1: Multiple moving effects of whatever is in front of the camera will be displayed as soon as you start up the app. It is so easy to use

## Time for photo fun

Photo Booth will keep you and your friends amused for ages

### Use it to:

- **Apply multiple effects at once**
  The main screen shows nine effects at a time.

- **Capture the moment**
  You can capture any effect with the tap of a button.

- **Manipulate the effects**
  You can manipulate each effect with your fingers.

- **Share the effects**
  You can share effects by email or add them to your contacts.

- **Show a different view**
  Both cameras can be used to create fun effects.

### Fun photo effects

Photo Booth does only one thing, but it does it very well. With almost no effort at all, you can create silly and amusing effects and keep them forever. When you start the app, you are presented with a screen that is split into nine parts, and you will see different effects in each section (see Fig 1). The middle one shows the normal view but the craziness happens in all of the surrounding squares. When you tap a square, it will pop up full screen and you can view the effect in all its glory.

The apps works so quickly that it would be easy to just accept whatever image effect is on the screen and capture it. But if you take your time to play around and get a feel for the all of the many effects, the results can be useful for anything from photos, to posters, to still special effects for school projects (Figs 2 and 3). You can also hit the camera switch icon at the bottom and take photos of anything that is in front of you. When you snap landscapes and wider shots, you will see the ability to create some effects that otherwise would take a lot of time to create via the editing process.

Fig 2: Some of the effects are completely bizarre so take your time to get used to them and capture them as you want

Fig 3: Don't just accept whatever image you're presented with on the screen. Perfect it for the project you have in mind

"With some time spent making sure that the effect is well placed, you can use the image for posters"

Fig 1: Photo Booth images can be shared via email by tapping two options in your camera roll

# "Add a Photo Booth image to a contact, and it'll be displayed when they email you"

## Share your photos

The amusing effects you capture are fun on their own, but the fun can be shared with others very easily. When you capture a photo in Photo Booth, it is immediately saved in your Camera Roll and the results can be instantly shared. If you tap the top-right icon, you can then tap any photo to bring up a new menu. If you tap the email option, a new email will pop up and you can then send it immediately (Fig 1). You can alternatively tap the 'Tweet' option (if you have a Twitter account) and it will be added to a new Tweet at which point you can add your own comment explaining

the bizarre image you are publishing (Fig 2). Photo Booth interacts with the Camera Roll which in turn interacts with Twitter, email services, wireless printers and SMS services.

It is also possible to add a Photo Booth image to one of your contacts by navigating to a specific contact and then tapping the 'add photo' option (Fig 3). This will then let you choose any captured image which will be shown if that particular contact calls or emails you. You will likely want to add a regular photo for professional contacts, but for some people a Photo Booth image may feel more funnily appropriate.

Fig 2: Tweeting Photo Booth images is as quick and convenient as any other system and even faster than most

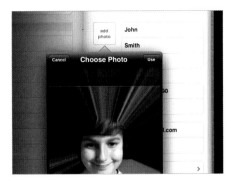

Fig 3: Adding Photo Booth images to contacts is great fun, especially if the person is not one of your favourite people

## Change with a touch
Make every Photo Booth effect completely unique

### 1: Change the original effect

The original effect may not be as flattering as you like, but all you need to do to change it is touch the iPad's touch screen in a few different ways.

### 2: Highlight a particular section

Drag your finger around the screen to see how your image changes in real time. Our top tip: you get the best results with faces!

### 3: Stretch the effect

By using two fingers in the standard 'pinch' motion you can stretch certain effects to make them even more pronounced than before.

### 4: Use your imagination

Instead of altering the focal point, you can stretch the surrounding parts of the image to make the focal point seem even smaller.

# Game Center

Sign in to Game Center and connect with your friends for online gaming, score comparisons and achievements to boost your gamer score. We present you everything you need to know

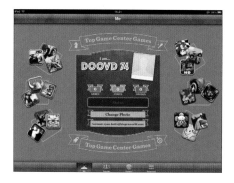

## Use it to:

- **Play games**
  Set up games to play online with your friends.

- **Make friends**
  Meet new iOS gamers and meet up for sessions.

- **Find games**
  Discover new games with in-app recommendations.

- **Earn achievements**
  Earn rewards for your gaming prowess.

- **Compare scores**
  See how your scores match those of your friends.

- **Make new buddies**
  Befriend friends of friends to widen your network.

*Fig 1 (top left): Choose a photo from Photos to stare out from your profile page*

*Fig 2 (main image): Once you are signed in, give yourself a nickname and choose whether to go public*

*Fig 3 (bottom left): Add text to your status and setup's complete*

# It's play time!

## Discover a new world of gaming at your fingertips

### Setting up Game Center

Originally released with iOS 4.1, Apple's Game Center services has been tweaked and enhanced in subsequent updates to become a fully-fledged gaming portal with iOS 5 and 6. Free to use, Game Center serves many purposes. Primarily it allows you to link up with your friends, trade scores and achievements, and set up multiplayer games so that you can compete against your friends online. It is also a great way to discover new games for your device – either through seeing what your friends are playing or via recommendations through the service. Setting up your own personal Game Center is easy. When you first

launch the app the first thing you will be required to do is sign in using your Apple ID – the same email address and password you use for your iTunes account.

Next you will be required to enter a Nickname, which is made public and will appear in leaderboards and multiplayer games (see Fig 2). Select whether you want your profile to be made public and then tap the 'Done' button. To apply the final slithers of personality to your profile, you can tap on the Status box to enter some text (Fig 3). Then add a photo to sit menacingly on your Game Center Home screen (Fig 1). Once your profile has been set up, you're ready to start playing!

Fig 1: Go to the 'Requests' section to start adding friends to your Game Center

## Game Center Friends

Making friends through Game Center is easy, simply tap on the 'Requests' icon at the bottom of the screen and then tap on 'Add Friends' (Fig 1). You will then be prompted to enter the email address or nickname of the friend you wish to add, after which a friend request will be sent to them to consider, accept or deny (Fig 2). When you receive a friend request you will be alerted by a push notification and the request will appear on this screen for you to accept or deny.

Once you have accepted friend requests, or they have accepted your requests, tap on the 'Friends' icon at the bottom of the screen and your friends will be displayed as a list down the left-hand side of the screen. Tap on a

friend and various pieces of information will be displayed underneath their profile, including the number of Game Center compatible games they own, their gamer score (calculated by the achievements that they have earned) and their number of friends. You can also see at-a-glance which games you have in common and also view games that they own and you don't, so you can download them to your iPad, yourself, and start competing against your friend (Fig 3).

Also presented at the top of your friends list on the 'Friends' screen is a 'Recommendations' section. Tap on this to get a list of friends associated with other people on your friends list whom you haven't befriended yourself yet – so start sending out those requests.

Fig 2: Tap on 'Add Friends' and then enter their email address or nickname to invite them

Fig 3: Tap on friends on your list to see what they're playing, and compare games and scores

## Add a friend
Invite your friends to get the most out of Game Center

### 1: Go to 'Requests'
In the main window, tap the 'Requests' icon at the bottom of the screen.

### 2: Add friends
Next, tap on the 'Add Friends' link in the middle of the screen.

### 3: Send request
Enter the email address or nickname of your friend and add a message.

### 4: Check the list
When requests are accepted, your friends will be in the friends section.

## Your profile

The main 'You' screen of Game Center displays your nickname, photo, status and an overview of how many Game Center games you own, your overall score and your number of friends

## Top Game Center Games

The most popular Game Center compatible games are displayed around your profile. Tap on an icon to view them in the App Store

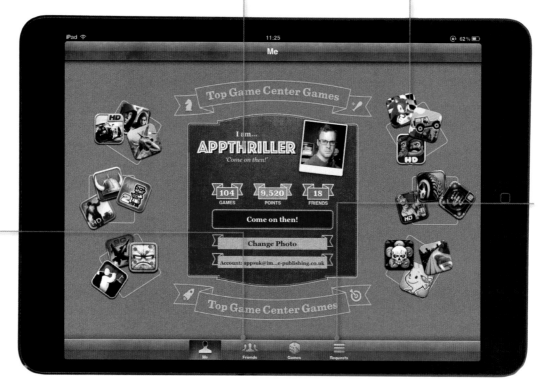

## Your friends

Tap the 'Friends' icon at the bottom of the screen to view your friends list and compare games and scores

## Requests

The 'Requests' icon will allow you to send friend requests to new friends and accept any requests that you may have been sent

## Achievements

Anyone who owns a PlayStation 3 or an Xbox 360 gaming console will be familiar with achievements. Achievements are awarded for completing special tasks within games and for each achievement you earn, you will be awarded points – which vary from achievement to achievement – that contribute to your overall Game Center score.

Not all Game Center games come with achievements, though most do, and you can view which games have achievements and, most importantly, what they are, by tapping on the 'Games' section icon which is present at the bottom of the screen.

Here you will be presented with an overview of all of the Game Center compatible games you have on your iPad (Fig 1) and, by tapping on a game you'll be able to view player leaderboards (if applicable), who on your friends list is playing the game, and the achievements available – use the tabs at the top of the window to access the 'Achievements' section (Fig 2). On this page

# "Achievements are awarded for completing special tasks within games"

you will be presented with the full list of achievements, each one comes with a brief, (sometimes cryptic) description of what you have to do to earn the achievement and the

number of points available. When you earn an achievement, you will be notified in the game and the applicable icon will be added to the relevant Achievements screen in Game Center.

*Fig 1: Tap the 'Games' icon to get an overview of all of the Game Center compatible games on your iPad*

*Fig 2: Tap on the 'Achievements' tab on a particular game to view all of the achievements earned and those you can still earn*

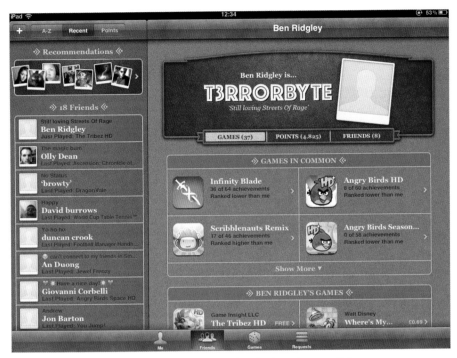

Fig 1: Check the 'Friends' section of Game Center to ensure that you and your friends own the same multiplayer games

Fig 2: Scroll to the bottom of 'Games' section to visit the App Store and find new online games

Fig 3: While in-game, tap on the multiplayer options to launch Game Center and invite your friends to play

## "Game Center allows you to play games and compete with random players"

### Playing online

A key feature of Game Center is the ability to play online multiplayer games against your friends. Obviously, you can only do this in games that support online multiplayer gaming, otherwise you'll have to be content with competing against your friends in the online leaderboards and achievement stakes. But once you have a Game Center compatible game that supports online play, and you have friends who have the same as well, setting up a match is easy (Fig 1).

To get started with online multiplayer, tap on the 'Games' icon in Game Center and scroll down to the 'Find Game Center Games' link. Tap this to be taken to the Game Center section of the App Store and browse the 'Online' section for games to buy (Fig 2). Once you have downloaded an online game, launch it, then locate the multiplayer online option in the game and tap it. Game Center will now kick in and allow you to invite games to play or auto-match you against a random opponent (Fig 3). Whatever option you pick, there is always someone online to play with. This sets the stage for a more personal, yet friendly, contest. All that's left is to enjoy hours of online gaming through Game Center.

## Find friends
Use the recommendations feature to find friends

### 1: Tap on Friends
On the Game Center screen, tap on the 'Friends' tab at the bottom of the screen.

### 2: See recommendations
At the top of your friends list is a section called 'Recommendations'; tap on this.

### 3: Review recommendations
On the list of friends of friends, tap on 'Send Friend Request' to any you know.

### 4: Use contacts
Scroll to the bottom and tap on 'Use My Contacts' to add friends from contacts.

# Edit your status
## Share your thoughts with your Game Center friends

## 1: Go to the 'Me' page
While in Game Center, tap on the 'Me' section from the options at the bottom.

## 2: Tap status
Tap on the status window in the middle of the screen and start typing.

## 3: Tap 'Done'
When you have finished typing, hit 'Done' to publish your status.

## 4: Share status
Your status will be visible to everyone in your friends list.

### Game screens
Tapping on individual games in the 'Games' section of Game Center will bring up a page dedicated to that game featuring all the essential info

### Online leaderboards
You can see how your performance stacks up against that of your friends and the Game Center community, at large, by tapping the 'Leaderboard' option

## Leaderboards

If you don't want to play against other gamers online, then there are others ways to boast about your superiority through Game Center – namely through the online leaderboards. Whenever you play a game, your score will be recorded and stored in Game Center, compared against those of your friends and stacked up against the rest of the Game Center community. To see this in effect, tap on the 'Games' section of Game Center (accessible from the icon at the bottom of the window), which will display all of the games that are installed on your iPad (and your other iOS devices if you are logged into the game

account on all of them) and then tap on one of the games displayed (Fig 1). There is plenty of information to digest on the page that appears. At the top will be your rank – both against your friends and every Game Center user who has played the game – and the achievements that you have earned - the total number and the total score they make up (Fig 2). Further down the page will be two leaderboards. The one on the left ranks you alongside your Game Center Friends and the one on the right shows the overall leaderboard of all players. You can filter the leaderboards by tapping on the 'Today', 'This Week' and 'All-Time' options at the top.

Fig 1: Tap on a game in the 'Games' section to see leaderboards for your friends and the Game Center community

Fig 2: Tap on the 'Total Score' option in order to get breakdowns of each score category for that particular game

## Game recommendations

Unless you study the App Store meticulously each day, chances are that new game releases may escape your notice from time to time. But with Game Center enabled you'll never miss the hottest new releases and the best multiplayer games. While in Game Center, tap on the 'Games' section and, displayed at the top of the screen will be a section called 'Game Recommendations' (Fig 1). Tap on this and you'll be presented with an extensive list of new game apps to buy and download.

Tap on a game in the recommendations section and you will see its main screen, as if it was already installed on your system. It will also include all of your friends who currently own and play that particular game (Fig 2). From this screen you can purchase the app and tell other friends about it. If you do decide to buy the app then tap on the price in the top-right corner and you'll be taken through to the app's main page in the App Store, whereby you can go through the transaction process as normal (Fig 3).

You can also get game recommendations from the 'Top Game Center Games' highlights in the 'Me' section. Surrounding your profile will be a host of game app icons. Tap on these to be enlightened about the most popular Game Center games of the moment.

## "With Game Center enabled, you'll never miss the hottest new releases"

Fig 1: Tap the 'Game Recommendations' section at the top of the Games page to get enlightened about possible new purchases

Fig 2: You will be taken to a screen of recommended games that you can purchase directly from Game Center

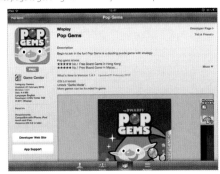

Fig 3: If you opt to buy a game then you'll be taken to that game's page in the App Store

## Game Center launch
### How to start games directly from Game Center

### 1: Go to Games
Go to the Games section of Game Center. Now tap the game you want.

### 2: Play Game
On the main game screen, tap the 'Play Game' option in the top-right corner.

### 3: Launch the game
The game you selected will now be launched from within Game Center.

### 4: Start playing
Launching games through Game Center is a quick way to get playing.

# Newsstand

With Newsstand, all the latest digital magazines will be delivered straight to your iPad every month for you to read on your device. Here we take an in-depth look at this wonderful service

## Use it to:

- **Buy magazines**
  Purchase and download digital magazines without leaving the house.

- **Shop for publications**
  There is a dedicated Newsstand section for this in the App Store.

- **Automatic deliveries**
  When a new issue is available, it will be delivered straight to your iPad.

- **Read in exciting ways**
  Enjoy numerous iPad enhancements that print media could never match.

- **Build a library**
  Take your entire magazine collection with you for convenient reading.

*Fig 1 (top left): Visit categories to see all of the publications that are available*

*Fig 2 (main image): Tap 'Store' in Newsstand to go straight to the Newsstand section of the App Store*

*Fig 3 (bottom left): Tap on a magazine or newspaper to visit its info page and read all about it*

# Reading digital media

Your iPad is a digital newsagent that delivers the latest issues of your favourite magazines and newspapers to your screen

## The Newsstand Store

When you first launch the Newsstand app, which was first released as part of the iOS 5 update, you'll be presented with empty virtual shelves. To fill them, visit the Newsstand Store and grab yourself some digital publications to peruse on your iPad.

Tap the 'Store' button in the top-right corner of the window and you'll be directed to the Newsstand section of the App Store, where you will be inundated with a choice of digital magazines and newspapers to download (see Fig 2). Special featured publications are advertised at the top of the screen. If one

interests you, tap on the flash ad to be taken to that magazine's information page (Fig 3).

Scroll down and the rest of the page will be broken down into sections, such as 'New & Noteworthy' (the latest magazines to be given the Newsstand treatment) and 'What's Hot'. Tap the 'See All' link next to a section header to view Newsstand apps that relate to that category, and then tap on an individual app to view its info page (Fig 1). From here, you can tap 'Install' and the publication will download and appear on your personal Newsstand shelves. From here you are able to tap to open it up and read at your own convenience.

*Fig 1: Tap on a publication on your Newsstand shelves to open it up and start reading*

## "Most digital publications offer free samples so you can browse first"

### Read and navigate a magazine

Reading on your iPad is an intuitive, natural experience that comes with its own digital benefits that you simply wouldn't get from reading a physical magazine. These include options to enhance the reading experience and, in some cases, interactive video and interactivity merged seamlessly into the make-up of the magazine.

As you will discover when downloading magazines and newspapers from the Newsstand Store, the main viewing portal through which you read the magazines is free, but when you launch the specific magazine from within Newsstand, you'll have to buy individual issues or take out a subscription so each new issue is delivered to your device.

Most digital publications offer free trials or sample issues, so you can browse through them on your iPad to gauge whether you like the content that it delivers (Fig 2). To read a magazine on your iPad, tap on its cover from the shelves and when the main page is displayed, tap anywhere on the screen (Fig 1). From the contents page you can tap on a feature to jump straight to it. Use your fingers to swipe up or down the page to read it, and left to right to turn the pages (Fig 3).

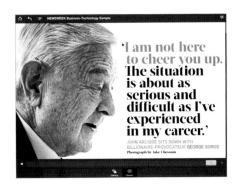

*Fig 2: You may have to buy or subscribe within the app, but most digital magazines offer free samples*

*Fig 3: Move your finger around the screen to access features, scroll through pages or turn pages*

## Delete a magazine
### Don't recycle old publications. Just delete them

### 1: Visit the library
Most magazines contain a library of your downloaded issues; tap on this.

### 2: Tap edit
Tap the 'Edit' button and then tap the symbol next to an issue to delete it.

### 3: Open Newsstand
To delete an entire mag app, start by opening Newsstand.

### 4: Tap the 'X'
Press and hold on a cover, then tap an 'X' above to the mag you're deleting.

# Newsstand

**Launching Newsstand**
Tap the Newsstand icon to launch the app and display your purchased and downloaded digital publications on rows of virtual shelves

**Your digital publications**
All of the mags you purchase and download will be laid out on virtual shelves. To open one, simply tap on its cover

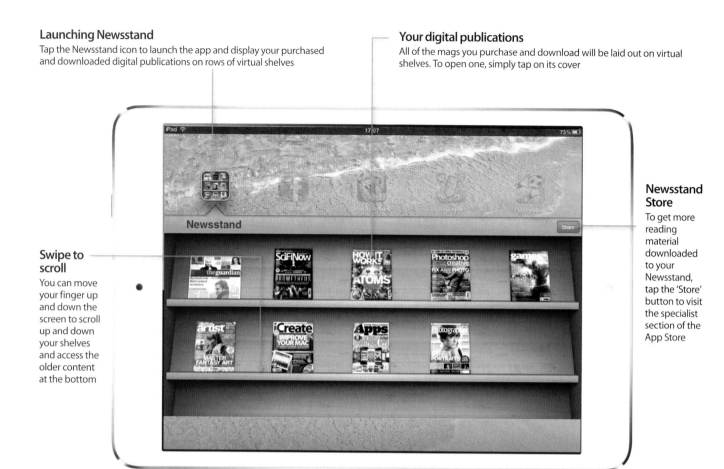

**Newsstand Store**
To get more reading material downloaded to your Newsstand, tap the 'Store' button to visit the specialist section of the App Store

**Swipe to scroll**
You can move your finger up and down the screen to scroll up and down your shelves and access the older content at the bottom

## Subscriptions

One of the best things about Newsstand is that it's convenient. As we have already explored, buying and reading newspapers and magazines through your iPad is easy, but things get easier still if you subscribe.

After downloading the app of a specific digital publication, that sits on your virtual Newsstand shelves, you can go into the app and set up a subscription using your regular iTunes account and billing data (Fig 3), after which every subsequent issue of that publication will be automatically delivered to your Newsstand app without you having to lift a finger (Fig 1). Don't worry if you haven't finished reading the last one as it will be stored within the app, but the new issue will take pride of place and you will be notified when a new issue has been delivered. Subscription rates are on the app's info page on the App Store (under 'Top In App Purchases'), or tap on the cover of a mag app to open it up from your Newsstand app and then tap on the latest issue. In many cases, the cost of a subscription will appear alongside the latest issue and you can tap on a price option to set up a subscription. The process varies between magazines, but just make sure you don't rush into anything without reading all of the available options (Fig 2).

*Fig 1: Details of subscription offers will most likely be apparent when you launch the respective mag apps*

*Fig 2: Make sure you read and understand all aspects of the subscription, and the costs involved, before committing*

*Fig 3: When you decide to take out a subscription, the cost price will be billed directly to your iTunes account*

## MAD MEH

### AMC'S FIRST REALITY SHOW, 'THE PITCH,' A BLAND LOOK AT THE AD WORLD

**BY EMMA BARKER**

"What's more dramatic than the 1960s advertising industry?" AMC executives evidently asked themselves when developing their new reality show on the coattails of their "Mad Men" success.

"Today's advertising industry!" was the probable response.

This was the first wrong turn.

"Mad Men" is compelling because of its gorgeous period sets and costumes and high-stakes personal drama. Analysis of the show cites themes of obsolescence, abandonment, identity and death. No one ever touts "Mad Men" as a

look inside the fast-paced world of advertising. Here's why: The world of advertising is not exciting. Do you have a white-collar job? Then you know what it's like!

In "The Pitch," adults sit in cubicles trying to think of things that teenagers will like. Talking food that makes bad puns? Word play? Viral videos? Rap, definitely rap. It's a reality show that's sort of a competition show. Each episode centers around one company auditioning two ad agencies for its latest campaign. Since each week features two new agencies, we form no emotional attachments to those

wrestling with their creative monsters. Not that we would anyway: Most of them are grating at best, slinging industry lingo and obsessing over the win.

The best part of "The Pitch," as it would be with any reality show about a certain industry, is the peek we get inside the offices that actually make the stuff we see on TV. Have you ever seen a commercial trying too hard to be fun-

ny, or one that's brutally mundane, and thought, "Who came up with that?" Well, now you know. Come to think of it, maybe "The Pitch" is more like "Mad Men" than we've given it credit for: It's an exploration of another period of ad executives struggling with obsolescence. ■

*"The Pitch" premieres Monday, at 9 p.m. Eastern, 8 p.m. Central on AMC.*

THE DAILY | WEDNESDAY, APRIL 25, 2012

*Fig 1: You will often see movies embedded into the pages. Simply tap to start playing*

## "Without the constraints of print media, publishers are make reading interactive"

### Interactive magazines

Perhaps the best thing about iPad magazines is their flexibility. Without the constraints of traditional print media, publishers can flex their creative muscles to make the reading experience truly memorable by embedding all manner of interactivity into the pages.

While reading a magazine on your iPad, you may notice embedded video to add weight and context to a story. Tap to play this video on the page without leaving the app (Fig 1). Likewise, you may encounter games that can be tied to your Game Center account (Fig 2), or sound clips to play, images to manipulate

and other assorted special effects that are seamlessly integrated into the reading experience and that you can manipulate with your finger to make the stories stand out. Some magazine spreads with text laid out over a double-page image may actually come to life before your very eyes, as the subject matter strolls into view on the page (Fig 3). There is no end to the possibilities and you'll want to download more and more digital publications just to see how far the boundaries can be pushed as publishing and technology join hands to take us on a thrilling journey to the next level of reading.

*Fig 2: It isn't uncommon now for games to be integrated into digital magazines*

*Fig 3: By pressing on certain images you will be able to scroll around and explore them further*

### 1: Download the mag
Visit the Newsstand Store and then download the desired mag app.

### 2: Launch the app
Launch Newsstand and then tap on the cover of the magazine.

### 3: Browse issues
From within the app, browse through all available issues and tap on one.

### 4: Tap to buy
Tap 'Buy' to purchase the magazine and download it to your library.

# iBooks

With the latest update announced in October 2012, iBooks 3.0 has some incredible new features to help you get the best reading experience on all of your Apple devices

## Use it to:

- **Buy and sample**
  You can purchase books and get free samples from a dedicated iBook Store.

- **Bookmark pages**
  Save multiple bookmarks for future use.

- **Scroll vertically**
  Change the way you read with a few simple steps.

- **Change the style**
  Change the font style and size to suit your tastes.

- **Share quotes**
  Share quotes you read via email and social networks.

- **Add notes**
  Highlight text and apply your own notes.

*Fig 1 (top left): The Store is crammed full of eye-catching propositions and categories*

*Fig 2 (main image): Access the Store from within the app by tapping 'Store' in the top-left*

*Fig 3 (bottom left): The 'Browse' section allows you to search via categories and even paid-for and free books*

# Reading on your iPad

Discover how you can access thousands of books and magazines and conveniently read them on your iPad

### The iBookstore

Amazingly, iBooks isn't a default iPad app. You have to download it from the App Store. Mercifully it's free, and most definitely an app that no avid reader should be without. To use iBooks you naturally need some reading material – and you can gather plenty of that from the iBooks Store. This section of the App Store, that is devoted to digital e-literature, can be accessed from within the iBooks app by tapping on the 'Store' button in the top-left corner of the screen (Fig 2). Once there you will be presented with a Featured section that showcases the significant new additions. Scroll down and you'll find sections dedicated to 'New & Notable' and 'New Bestsellers'.

But what if you just want something to try out the iBooks app and see if you can use it as a viable reading tool? Simple! Along the bottom of the screen are further sections. Tap on 'Top Charts' and you'll find a section full of free and paid books, the former you can download without spending a penny (Fig 1). The 'Top Authors' takes you to an alphabetical list of all the best-selling authors in paid and free formats (Fig 3), so it's easy to find something to read from pretty much any genre, when you want it.

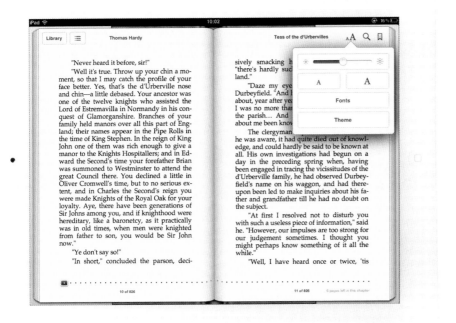

*Fig 1: The font icon lets you tailor the reading experience to suit your own preferences*

# "Give the pages a sepia tone or switch to night mode to read in low light"

## Navigating an eBook

When reading an eBook through the iBooks app, the reading interface will be packed full of options to tailor the experience to suit your own tastes and preferences.

If the book you're reading turns out to be not to your taste, there are options in the top-left corner of the interface to assist you. 'Library', enables you to swiftly exit the book and jump back to your book collection, while the list icon takes you to the contents page of the book. Then there are options to alter the appearance of the book. Tap on the font icon in the top-right corner of the page (Fig 1) and

you can move a slider to adjust the brightness, increase the size of the text, change the font and alter the theme.

The final options include a magnifying glass icon that lets you search for words or page numbers, and a bookmark icon to bookmark the current page. Double tap a word to select it and press words to select and highlight text and add notes (Fig 2). By going to iBooks in the Settings menu, you can activate the options to sync bookmarks and collections, show all purchases and allow your downloaded books to access publisher's content from the Internet (Fig 3).

*Fig 2: Press on words to highlight text and apply your own notes, which can be synced via iCloud*

*Fig 3: Go to the iBooks section in Settings to activate the options to sync bookmarks and collections over iCloud*

# Buy an eBook
## Purchasing books or getting free samples is easy

### 1: Find a book
Use the search bar to quickly find a book by its title or author.

### 2: Buy or sample
Tap the book to get a book description, price, sample, ratings and reviews.

### 3: Read sample
If you choose to get a sample, it will be downloaded to your collection.

### 4: Buy later
If you enjoy the sample, the option to buy the full book will end the preview.

# iBooks

## Your books

All of your downloaded books and samples will appear on virtual shelves within the iBooks app. Tap on a cover to open and start reading the book

## Collections

You can organise your books into collections by tapping the 'Collections' button, creating a new collection and then tapping 'Edit' to move your books

## Views

You can change how your books are displayed by either opting for the default, shelf view or switching to a list

## Edit

The 'Edit' button lets you select books to move to various collections or delete books that are in your library

## Read ePub files and PDFs directly from Mail

As well as allowing you to read books, the iBooks app is also a useful utility that enables you to open and read ePub files and PDFs. This is especially handy if you receive these files as email attachments because you can choose to open them in iBooks from within the Mail app and store them in your library.

To open an ePub file or PDF from Mail, tap on the attachment in your email and a menu will appear with options to have a 'Quick Look' at the file, 'Open in iBooks' or open it in some other app (Fig 1). Choose the iBooks option and, if the attachment is an ePub file, it will be added to your book library and automatically open in iBooks. When opening a PDF attachment, the file will be added to a section in iBooks called 'PDFs' and, again, will open automatically (Fig 2). To access your saved PDF files from within iBooks later, launch the app and then, from your library, swipe left across the screen to access the PDF section and then simply tap on a PDF to open it (Fig 3). While viewing PDFs through iBooks, you will get all of the options available to you as if you were reading a book except for the option to change the size and style of the font.

## "You can read ePub files and PDFs in iBooks. This is handy if you receive these files as email attachments"

Fig 1: Press and hold on an attached file and choose the 'Open in iBooks' option

Fig 2: PDF files will be opened from within iBooks and you can pinch to zoom and utilise many more options

Fig 3: Swipe left from your iBooks library page to access a new page where your PDFs are stored

iBooks

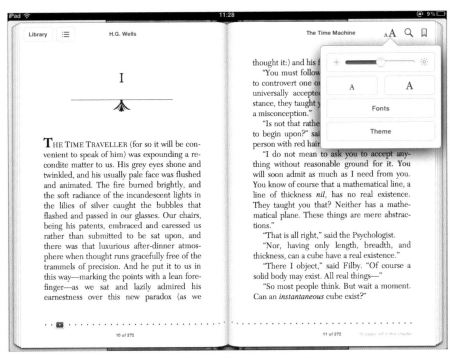

*Fig 1: You can start customising your reading experience by tapping the font icon in the top-right corner*

# "Adjust the brightness of the screen to make it easier on the eyes"

## Customise eBooks

Unlike actual physical books, you can manipulate those that you read through iBooks to tailor the reading experience to your own circumstances. For example, you can adjust the brightness of the screen to make it easier on the eyes, increase the size and the style of font to make it easier to read and change the theme to suit your current environment and reading conditions.

These options can be applied by tapping the font icon in the top-right corner of the screen while reading a book (Fig 1). This will bring up a menu of options, at the top of

which is a slider that you can move with your finger to adjust screen brightness. Under this are two buttons indicating different sizes of font. The default size is indicated by the smaller of the two 'A's, but you can increase the size by tapping the larger 'A'. (Fig 2) As this will cause less text to be visible on the pages, the page numbers will be removed.

If you want to change the font entirely then tap on the 'Fonts' option and pick a suitable font from the eight options provided. Finally, you can change the theme by tapping the 'Theme' button and picking one of the three available options (Fig 3).

*Fig 2: You can change the size of the font and, indeed, the font itself by choosing the applicable options*

*Fig 3: Why not experiment with different themes? How about a sepia tint or the low-light night mode*

# Scroll vertically
## Scroll vertically for continuous text flow

### 1: Tap the font icon
While reading, tap the font icon in the top-right corner.

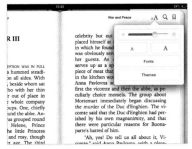

### 2: Tap on Theme
From the options, tap the 'Theme' button which reveals a drop-down.

### 3: Switch to scroll
Select the last option 'Scroll'. This is the latest new feature with iBooks 3.0.

### 4: Free Flow
You can now scroll down to have smooth flowing text as you read.

# Share quotes
## Share quotes with the latest version of iBooks

## 1: Select a word
Double tap a (big) word in the quote/sentence you want to share.

## 2: Select your sentence
Highlight the sentence by manually adjusting the length of the pointers.

## 3: Click Share
If the Share option does not come up, tap the highlighted sentence.

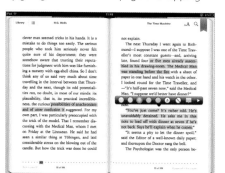

## 4: Chose sharing platform
Share this quote via Mail or social media – as long as you have active accounts.

## Your reading interface
Reading through iBooks is easy. Simply swipe left or right across the screen to turn the pages or move the slider at the bottom to skim through the book

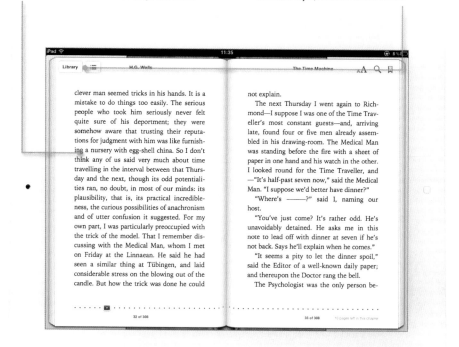

## Reading options
Tap the icons at the top of the screen to go to the library, jump to the contents, change the font and style, and search for words

## Reading tools
One of the best features of iBooks is the way in which you can bookmark multiple pages, highlight chunks of text and add in your own notes – perfect if you are using iBooks as a revision tool and need to make notes and highlight key sections for future reference.

It's all easy to do thanks to the remarkably intuitive interface of iBooks. While you're reading, if you need to stop or just fancy marking the page to refer back to later, tap the bookmark icon that's located in the top-right corner of the screen to save the page. You can then refer back to your bookmarks later by going to the contents page and tapping

on the 'Bookmarks' tab. You can also highlight text by pressing your finger down on the first word of the passage you want to highlight and then dragging your finger across. When you take your finger off the screen a new bar of options will appear (Fig 1) that will allow you to change the highlight colour (or opt for an underline style instead), remove the current highlight and even add a note (these too can be accessed by tapping the 'Notes' tab at the top of the contents page) (Fig 2). By sliding your finger across to the arrow, it is also possible to reveal options to 'Define' or 'Search', saving you the time of manually entering the words into the search field.

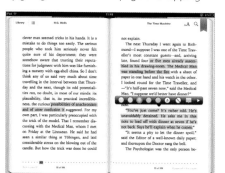

*Fig 1: Drag your finger across text to highlight it and bring up a new floating bar of options*

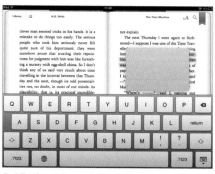

*Fig 2: Tap the note icon on the bar to add a note, which will be saved for future reference*

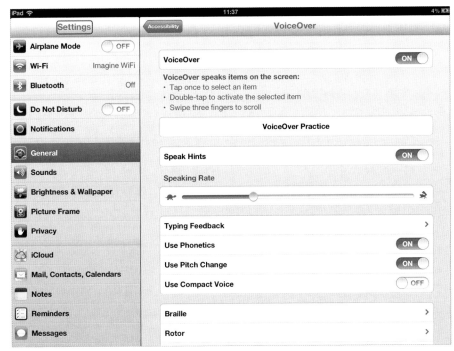

*Fig 1: Go to the Accessibility section of General Setting to set Voiceover to 'On'*

# "Rather than download an extra audio book, let your iPad read your book to you"

## Using VoiceOver

eBooks and audio books are completely separate entities as far as your iPad is concerned. If you want your books read to you then you would normally have to visit the iTunes Store and purchase the audio version, regardless of whether you already own the iBooks version of the same book. But there is a simple solution to prevent you from having to pay out twice for the same book if you want to listen to it – VoiceOver.

To start using this handy feature, launch your Settings app and go to the 'General' section. Scroll down to the 'Accessibility' section and then you will see an option

called 'VoiceOver'. Tap on this and set it to 'On', then go back to iBooks and start reading a book (Fig 1). While on a page, press the Home button three times and the option to 'Turn VoiceOver On' will appear (Fig 2). Select this, tap once on a page of text and then drag two fingers down the page to activate auto-reading and get your iPad to read the text to you using text to speech (Fig 3). This is by no means perfect, as the voice is quite robotic and lacks character and expression, but it works nevertheless. You can pause and resume VoiceOver by tapping two fingers on the screen and cancel it by triple-clicking the Home button again.

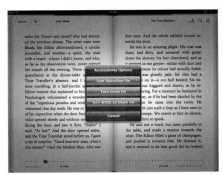

*Fig 2: While reading, simply triple-click Home in order to turn on VoiceOver*

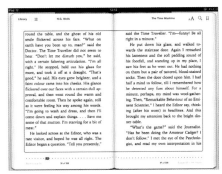

*Fig 3: Tap on the text and drag two fingers down the page to command your iPad to read to you*

## Add a bookmark
### Add a bookmark to pick up from where you left off

### 1: Tap bookmark
While reading, tap the fonts icon in the top-right corner.

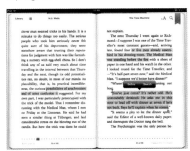

### 2: Add bookmark
A red bookmark graphic will then indicate that the page has been saved.

### 3: Your bookmarks
Go to the contents page and tap the 'Bookmarks' tab to access your pages.

### 4: Tap to access
Tap on a bookmark from the list to jump straight to that page.

# Pages

It may be an inexpensive app, but that is no indication of its quality. Pages is incredibly powerful, allowing you to produce outstanding letters and reports, with the ability to save them to iCloud

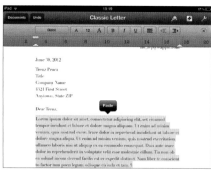

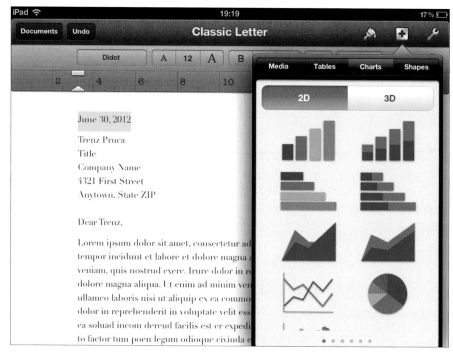

## Use it to:

- **Employ templates**
  Get a professional look from the start.

- **Add photos**
  Bring documents to life by adding images.

- **Dictate text**
  Speak your words rather than type.

- **Include movies**
  Take word processing to animated levels.

- **Resize simply**
  Pinch to rotate and drag to move.

- **Auto save**
  Never worry about losing your work.

- **Tap format**
  Tweak spacing and columns with ease.

*Fig 1 (top left): Alter the displayed fonts of your document. There are lots of options to choose from*

*Fig 2 (main image): You can add a variety of media including a set of charts that you can have both in 2D or 3D formats*

*Fig 3 (bottom left): The cut, copy and paste options are available. Just hold your finger on the text to highlight it*

# Create great work

**Produce stunning documents with ease using Apple's intuitive and feature-laden word processor**

### Create letters, reports and flyers

With a simple tap of the '+' icon in the corner of the iPad screen, you can start creating some amazing documents. Straight away, Pages lets you choose from a list of templates as well as a blank canvas and, once you are done, you can get to work immediately.

Pages displays a number of on-screen options (see Fig 3). You can alter the font of your text by tapping on the current font and selecting a new one from an exhaustive list (Fig 1). You can also increase or decrease the size of a font by altering the size number or by pressing the two A buttons on either side, one of which is smaller than the other. Pages also lets you add embolden, italicise and underline fonts using the on-screen icons at the top of the document. You can tap a button to justify your text left, centre, right or in full as well. All of this makes the app brilliant but it's the extra stuff which makes it the perfect tool for reports and flyers.

By tapping the '+' icon on a document, you can add photos, tables, charts and shapes to make your work more appealing (Fig 2). Each calls up a variety of options – for example the ability to choose the number of columns and rows in a table, grab a bar or pie chart, or use a triangle or square. When positioned on the page (making good use of the on-screen ruler to line them up), you can quickly create good-looking, professional work.

*Fig 1: There's a variety of pre-loaded templates available. Whether you're creating a formal letter or project proposal, it'll look fabulous*

# "Simply tapping on the text in Pages allows you to make alterations to it"

## Apple-designed templates

To make life easier and to speed up the creation process, Apple has included 15 templates and one blank canvas which is available every time you create a new document (Fig 1). Among them are four letters: modern photo, classic, format and personal photo. The actual text format of the letter is the same in each instance but the app adds different letterhead styles.

Altering one of these letters is easy (Fig 2). Each changeable image carries an icon. Tap it and you can cut, copy, delete or replace it. Tapping 'Replace' calls up your camera roll.

Just look through your images and choose the one you want. It will directly replace the existing image. Use your fingers to then alter the size and use two fingers to change the angle. Tapping on the text also enables you to make alterations (Fig 3). A single tap is all it needs to highlight an entire block.

As well as the letters, you can also choose from two resumes, a project proposal, term paper, visual report, poster, syllabus, party invite, thank you card, recipe and flyer. They are very well designed to cater for specific area of interest and the templates mean it will take no time at all to alter them.

*Fig 2: You don't have to follow the template exactly as it is laid out. Play around with the style to customise it to your needs*

*Fig 3: Tapping on sections of a template will highlight the entire part so that you can quickly remove or manipulate bits at will*

## Find and replace
### Replace a weak word by a stronger one

### 1: Call up the menu
Select the spanner icon, select Find in the menu and a search bar appears.

### 2: Select Find and Replace
Tap settings, select Find and Replace. Type your word and the replacement.

### 3: Change the word
Pages will highlight all mentions of the word. Tap 'Replace' to change. it.

### 4: Check out alternatives
Use arrows to see other incidences of the word. Tap each word for alternatives.

# Pages

## Tool bar
The main toolbar has all of the elements you need to put documents together including bold, italics, justify and fonts

## Spanner
The spanner icon, when pressed, lets you search for text, print or share your work and set up your document

## Paintbrush
Selecting the Paintbrush icon will call up fonts and their size, paragraph and text styles for easy one-tap changes

## Keyboard
The keyboard appears when you tap on any sections of text to allow you to make changes to the document

## Work with images

A large part of the Pages experience is bringing images side-by-side with words. If you are using a template, you can tap on an image and replace it with one from your camera roll and while the app automatically replaces the picture at the same size, there are other alterations you can make.

Double-tap an image to call up the Mask feature. This allows you to move the image

around and position it within the frame (Fig 1). You may have a picture of two people but only need to include a headshot of one. This feature lets you zoom in close enough to focus on just one person in the picture.

Clicking on the Paintbrush icon at the top of the screen shows you numerous photo style options (Fig 2). You can have the image in a solid frame, or reflected, or with a solid black border, for instance. It is also possible to alter

the thickness of the border by tapping Style Options. Doing this will give you many more border options and the ability to change the scale and style of the border, giving it a dotted appearance if you wish.

Tapping effects within the Paintbrush menu lets you toggle Shadow on and off. You can do the same with reflection. Finally, by sliding the opacity option you can change the solid nature of the image you are working with.

*Fig 1: The Mask option lets you position your images so that you can bring in more or less of it*

*Fig 2: Tapping the Paintbrush icon calls up a range of style options for your image's borders of which there is an extensive choice*

*Fig 3: Tap Arrange to move images to the front or flip them vertically or horizontally. You can also choose to wrap your text*

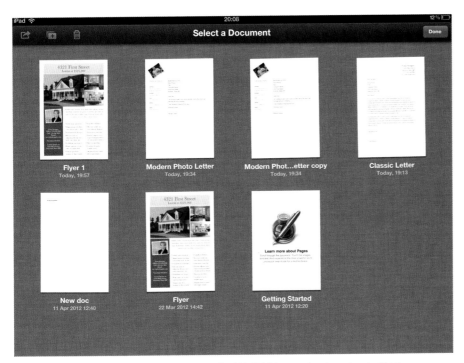

*Fig 1: Tap Edit on the main home screen and your documents will wobble. Highlight one and tap the trash can to delete it*

# "You can work with Pages on a Mac, iPhone and iPod touch"

## Work, save your progress and undo across devices

Pages works in conjunction with iCloud, Apple's cloud-based service that allows you to save documents to a remote server. In order to access this, you must go into Settings on your iOS device and turn the iCloud service on, allowing documents and data to be shared too (Fig 2). If you have a Mac, you can do the same here, under System Preferences.

Since you can work with Pages on a Mac, iPhone and iPod touch, this will let you access whatever work you do within Pages on any other system that has the Pages software,

making it a very versatile system. When you work with the app, your documents are automatically saved and, if you have iCloud turned on, they are also synced with the cloud too. There is, therefore, no save function within Pages. All of your completed documents are displayed when you start the app each time. Click Edit and you will see the documents wobble. You can now select them for deletion (Fig 1). You can also click the '+' icon to make a duplicate copy.

To open an older document, just tap it. As you work, you can correct mistakes by simply tapping the Undo button (Fig 3).

*Fig 2: In order to access the cloud, you need to have iCloud turned on within your iPad's Settings menu*

*Fig 3: There is an Undo button within Pages that you can activate whenever you make a mistake on a document*

## Export to .doc
### Produce a Word document from Pages

### 1: Write your document
When you are in a document, select the spanner icon when you want to export.

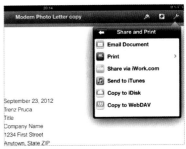

### 2: Your export selection
Tap on Share and Print and you will see a number of options.

### 3: Email a document
Tap on Email Document and you can choose a file format.

### 4: Select a Word document
To save a .doc file, you can select Word. You could also choose Pages or PDF.

# Pages

## Make a list
### Bullets or numbers?
### You can list your items

### 1: Open/create a document
Open a document and then go to where you want the list.

### 2: Type a number or letter
Now type either number 1 with a dot and space (ie '1. ') or a letter ('A. ').

### 3: Type and tap return
After the first entry, tap return. The next number/letter will automatically appear.

### 4: Finish your list
Press return twice. Tap the Paintbrush and select 'List' to change the style.

## Document Setup
You can use the Document Setup feature (accessed via the Spanner icon) to create a bespoke Pages document on your iPad

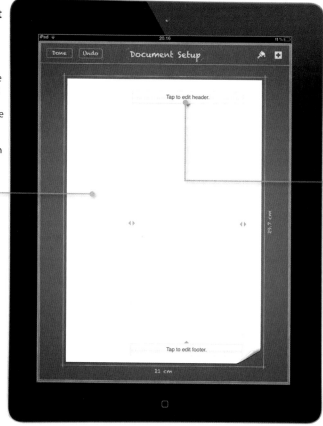

## Header and footer
Tapping on the header and footer parts of your document will allow you to make alterations for your freshly created template

## Share your work to iTunes, email and iWork.com
Although there is no save function with Pages and your work is automatically stored on your iPad, there will come a time when you will want to export it. This will allow you to send it to other people, which is handy if you're working on a school project or a document for work that needs approval.

Click on the Spanner icon and select Share and Print in order to see the export options built into Pages. You can email your document as a .doc or in Pages or PDF format. You can also send it in these formats to iTunes (Fig 1).

It requires you to connect your iPad to your computer. When you click the Apps tab in iTunes, your work will appear.

You can also share it via iWork.com (Fig 2). This is a service by Apple which is still in development as we write. Pressing the iWork option under the Spanner menu will prompt you to sign in using your Apple ID and password. Once done, you will be able to share your iWork documents with anyone who owns a Mac or PC. You can access the service online at iWork.com. If you have an iDisk login, this is another option open to you. Again tap on the Spanner but choose the iDisk option.

*Fig 1: Documents can be sent in PDF, Word or Pages format to iTunes. They will appear in the Apps tab*

*Fig 2: Use your Apple ID to sign up for iWork and share your work via this new Apple service*

Fig 1: The Print option is contained within the Spanner menu when you go to Share and Print

# "As long as your printer is on your Wi-Fi network, your iPad will look for it"

## Print with AirPrint

With AirPrint, you can print wirelessly from your iPad. It requires you to have an AirPrint-enabled printer and you can see a list of compatible devices by going to: http://store.apple.com/uk/browse/home/shop_mac/mac_accessories/printers?n=airprint&s=topSellers.

Setting up is easy. As long as your printer is on your Wi-Fi network, it will scan and look for compatible printers. It works in the background, too, so you can just get on with your task at hand while the printer does its magic. Pages has an AirPrint facility built in to it, as do many apps nowadays. By tapping on

the Spanner icon in the top right-hand corner of the screen, you are able to select Print among the many other options (Fig 1). This will bring up the Printer Options window and it will show any compatible printers (Fig 2).

As well as printers, other services may appear, especially if you use a wonderful piece of Mac software called Printopia which lets you print from an iPad without having an AirPrint printer (Fig 3). The Printer Options window also allows you to tell it how many copies you want. Use your finger to toggle the plus and minus signs. When you have finished, tap Print and the iPad will communicate wirelessly with your printer.

Fig 2: The Printer Options will show printers that the iPad has found on your network, and it will let you print

Fig 3: A package called Printopia will let you print to other devices, such as a PDF, straight to your Mac's screen

## Dictate your work
### Don't tap the screen when you can speak instead

**1: Tap your microphone**
To input text, instead of typing, tap the microphone button on the keyboard.

**2: Speak to your iPad**
An alert sounds to tell you to start talking. Press the mic button to stop.

**3: And as if by magic…**
The words will appear on the screen. It is quite accurate but you can edit the text.

**4: Edit the document**
Tap on the text and make alterations, if you wish, in the normal way.

# Numbers

Numbers is Apple's answer to Microsoft Excel, but it's friendlier and potentially more flexible. Here we show you how to get to grips with the ultimate iPad spreadsheet app

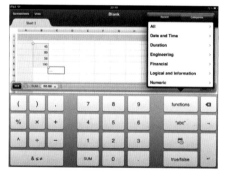

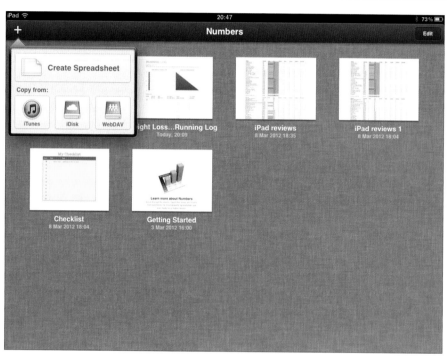

## Use it to:

- **Create with templates**
Pre-configured spreadsheets designed for various tasks.

- **Include mixed media**
Numbers can cope with photos and shapes.

- **Export**
Spreadsheets can be saved in PDF and Excel format.

- **Utilise all functions**
Includes all common Excel functions.

- **Design without grids**
Lack of a grid in most templates looks cleaner.

- **Make full use of graphs**
A selection of 2D and 3D graph styles are included.

- **Troubleshoot**
A full help guide is available with one tap.

*Fig 1 (top left): Double-tap any cell to bring up the data panel. Here, use the four icons at the top to input values*

*Fig 2 (main image): Tap the '+' icon to create a spreadsheet. A set of templates will appear*

*Fig 3 (bottom left): The functions panel has a detailed and varied list of functions*

# Facts and figures in style

Creating your spreadsheets with Numbers is more natural than with most similar apps

## Creating spreadsheets

The process of creating your first spreadsheet in Numbers starts with the tap of an icon, the '+' icon in the top left-hand corner which is visible in Fig 2. When you tap this you will be presented with a set of pre-configured templates, but it is best to start with the blank template. Choose this and you will see a simple grid of squares as you would expect with any spreadsheet app. Double tap a square and you will then see a new panel pop up, which you can see in Fig 1. There are four icons to choose from – numbers, date and time, text, and functions.

From these you can use the touch screen to quickly input the values you want in each cell. You can use the grey cells at the top and on the left as descriptors for your data. This is all the basic information you need to know to input the information you need.

Select a blank cell, go to the functions panel and then select a few cells with your finger as you can see in Fig 3. They will automatically be added together and you can also tap the functions icon in order to choose from a list of multiple functions, which is highly detailed and should cover every variable you require.

# Numbers

Fig 1: The template previews offer enough detail for you to decide if they will work for the task at hand

# "No matter what you want to do, chances are that there will be a template available"

## Apple-designed templates

Templates are one of the features that differentiates Numbers from competitor apps, and there are 16 pre-loaded ones to choose from here (Fig 1). You can pick from a simple checklist to more complex employee schedules and personal savings templates that can then be tweaked and customised to your exact needs. Apple has been careful not to over-fill each template with data but to still make it obvious how each part works – this should help you to get off to a flying start. When you open a template, it's not obvious at first that it's even a spreadsheet thanks to

the lack of a grid or labels at the top and side, but this method works perfectly for marrying graphs, data and images together (Fig 2).

The templates also have pre-configured formatting for each area so you need only worry about adding your new data and making the visual changes you want to (Fig 3). No matter what you want to do with each one, chances are that there will be a template available that will help you create a spreadsheet you need with minimal changes. It is amazing how much time a small selection of templates will save you if you use them wisely.

Fig 2: Almost all of the built-in templates look nothing like spreadsheets, but they most certainly are

Fig 3: The formatting for each part of a template has already been input so you only need to add and change the data

## Manage cells
You can modify and move every cell by touch alone

### 1: Tap cells to modify them
Double-tap a cell and a panel pops up allowing you to change the data.

### 2: One touch to start
Hold your finger on a cell and a dialog box pops up. Choose the 'Cut' option.

### 3: Move cells with cut/paste
Hold your finger on another cell and choose 'Paste' from the dialog box.

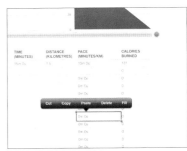

### 4: Delete a cell
Holding a finger down gives a 'Delete' option. Simply tap it to delete the cell.

# Numbers

**Your spreadsheets**
All of your spreadsheets, including previews, are available via the main page, which is accessible via this button

**Adding media**
You can add photos and other media by tapping the '+' button when in a particular cell or location

**Adding graphs**
Graphs can be created, in 2D and 3D, and placed anywhere simply by moving them around with your finger

**Manage your cells**
Cells can be managed by touch. Long taps and quick taps will instruct Numbers to expect different objectives

## Intelligent tables and keyboard

The keyboard in Numbers for iPad is not just a keyboard, it is intuitive and is able to understand exactly what you're doing. If you double-tap a cell which has a date in it, the keyboard will pop up with the date/time panel so that you can make immediate adjustments. It will pop up with the appropriate panel no matter what you already have in a cell and will even guess what you want to input into a blank cell in a column – an example is shown in Fig 1.

There is also a selection of prebuilt tables included in Numbers (Fig 2), which you can pick from and then add to any spreadsheet. You can resize them with just your finger and move them around as needed (Fig 3) and the software will learn what you want to put into each column and row as you build up the sheet. You might not even notice that it's happening, but the more you input, the cleverer the software becomes – you may even get to the point where the spreadsheets almost fill themselves.

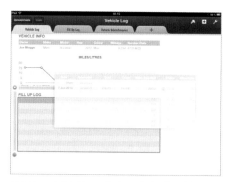

*Fig 1: When you double-tap a cell in a column, the software will guess which format you want to input your data in*

*Fig 2: Simply tapping the '+' button will pop up a dialog box which lets you insert pre-configured tables with ease*

*Fig 3: Move whole tables by selecting multiple cells and then holding your finger down. This lets you move it where you need to*

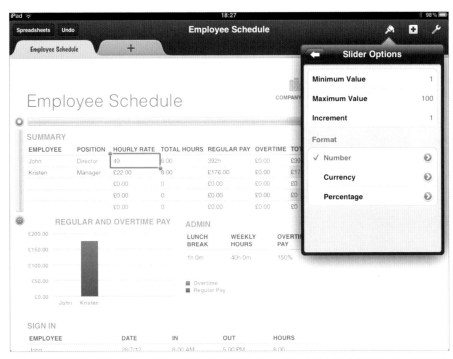

Fig 1: Sliders make projecting future values incredibly easy because you can change individual values for all of your data through one cell

# "Pop-up menus let you add information and data to a particular cell"

## Sliders, steppers and pop-ups

There are many other touch features available in Numbers, and sliders is a good example. Open a cell and the tap the paint brush. Choose 'Slider' from the Format list and then input a minimum and maximum value (Fig 1). When you next double-tap that cell, a slider will pop up and you can use your finger to change the value, which will conversely change the values in other cells. This is useful when dealing with changeable data.

If your data can change, but only in set increments, you can use steppers, which are available from the same place as the sliders.

It is possible to set the increments and also the exact format which should make it much easier to project figures in the future, as shown in Fig 2.

Also available are the pop-up menus, which let you add information and data to a particular cell. Use the same dialog box that you used previously and then choose 'Pop-Up Menu' from the list. You can then input data which will be displayed in the future when you double-tap the cell, as shown in Fig 3. These three simple features will save you lots of time and make your spreadsheets far cleaner, neater and organised.

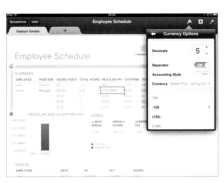

Fig 2: Steppers let you change the value of a cell in specific increments, which is a simple but effective time saver

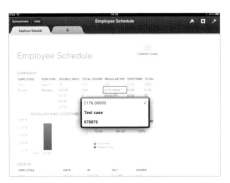

Fig 3: Pop-Up Menus can be used in a variety of ways to add information to cells without clogging up the main interface

## Export as .xls
Export your Numbers spreadsheets in Excel format

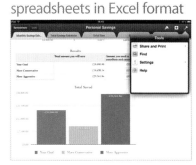

### 1: Start exporting
Tap the spanner icon top-right, then choose 'Share and Print' from the list.

### 2: Share in a variety of ways
A box asks which format you want. Choose one by tapping it.

### 3: Make it Excel compatible
Tap the 'Excel' icon, and Numbers will then convert the spreadsheet.

### 4: Time to share
The spreadsheet can be shared in Excel format with most formatting intact.

# Numbers

## Make a 3D chart
### Create attractive 3D charts with just a few taps

### 1: Select the data you need
Hold your finger down and slide it until you have chosen all the data to include.

### 2: Start the charting process
Choose 'Create Chart' from the dialog box that pops up and tap the 3D option.

### 3: Choose the right look
Select from a huge variety of charts by swiping through blocks of designs.

### 4: Place your chart
Your chart will be automatically created and you can now place it anywhere.

## Multiple tabs
You can have as many tabs as you like within one spreadsheet. This is useful for splitting up lots of complex data

## Add new tabs
The '+' button can be used to add new forms or sheets whenever you need to create separate data

## Functions and formulae
There are hundreds of functions and formulae built in to Numbers. The only difficulty will be mastering the exact ones you need to use for your work (Fig 1). Double-tap a cell and then choose the '=' option from the icon row above the keyboard. When you tap it, you will see a functions button on the right which is the home of all you will need to start creating deep and informative spreadsheets and databases. Tap it and a list will pop up, which is broken down into various categories.

Choose the one you need and then scroll through the next list to choose the exact function you require. At this point you will then see a new dialogue appear above the keyboard that lets you specify the exact format required. As you will discover, if you choose duration you can choose from weeks, days and many other options.

When you input some data into the cell, it will automatically be formatted as you need. You can also add formulas by tapping the '=' icon and then choosing other cells. You could select a cell, tap the '+' button, select another cell and the two will be added together. It is highly visual and takes away a lot of the complex thought process involved (Fig 2).

*Fig 1: The number of functions included can be bewildering, but does cover the needs of every user*

*Fig 2: The '+' icon above the keyboard is home to some of the more complex work you will undertake with Numbers*

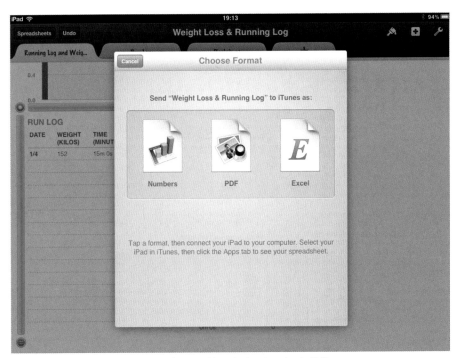

*Fig 1: All of your iOS devices can read and use Numbers spreadsheets that have been shared with iTunes*

# "Whether through iTunes, email or iCloud, sharing spreadsheets couldn't be easier"

## Sharing spreadsheets

Tap the spanner (top-right) and you will see the 'Share and Print' option window pop up. At this point you can choose to send a particular spreadsheet to iTunes. If your iPad is connected to a desktop or you can synchronise wirelessly, the document will be available to other Apple devices the next time they connect to iTunes (Fig 1).

You can also share via iWork.com, which is potentially easier. All this requires is to choose the option from the list and to then sign in with your Apple user ID and password as detailed in Fig 2. If you have not used iWork. com previously, you will be sent a verification

email. However, the service is moving to iCloud.com this year and so all spreadsheets that you currently share via the iWork option will now show up there instead.

It all works well, however, and is nothing but a name change. Sharing via email is as easy as the above two methods and requires choosing the Email option from the list and then choosing the format you want to send it in. The spreadsheet will be automatically added to an outgoing email (Fig 3) and all you then need to do is choose a recipient or recipients and add personalise your mail with some descriptive text. Sharing spreadsheets really couldn't be easier.

*Fig 2: iWork.com, which will soon be merging with iCloud, is an excellent way to ensure all of your devices are up to date*

*Fig 3: You can email a spreadsheet to anyone with a couple of taps and use a choice of formats*

## Add ratings
### Add some personality to your spreadsheets

### 1: Include star ratings
Double-tap a cell then the brush icon. Choose 'format' and then Star Rating.

### 2: Count the stars
The cell will now have 5 dots in it. Tap it 3 times to add 3 stars and so on.

### 3: Include some tickboxes
Follow the same process as step 1 and choose 'Tickbox' from the list.

### 4: Tick off your tasks
You can now include tasks to complete and tick them off with a single tap.

# Keynote

You can create a range of presentations that are, via the new iPad, more stunning than ever before - thanks to Retina display

Fig 1: Even though you work on one screen, you can always refer to other slides at a touch of a finger

Fig 2 (top left): A range of themes are on offer with others that can be created and stored on your iPad

Fig 3 (main image): Create a presentation or import the data from a variety of sources including iTunes, iDisk and WebDAV

## Use it to:

- **Create themes**
  Gives you a great start.

- **Tap to…**
  Organise and edit.

- **Combine media**
  Utilise varied apps to make your work look appealing.

- **Draw charts**
  Enhance your presentation with 3D charting.

- **Save**
  Save your work – while you work.

- **Make slideshows**
  Fancy transitions add class.

# Create a presentation

## Get started and be creative by opening and editing a new presentation project

### Create presentations across all devices

Enter the Presentations view and then tap the '+' button, situated in the top-left corner of the screen. As you can see from Fig 3 above, a number of options will appear but, for now, just press the 'Create Presentation' button. Don't be disturbed if the thumbnail images of your presentations fail to load when you open the app. This means that a presentation is already open from a previous session to be viewed or edited. Reset the screen and re-enter the thumbnail view by tapping the Presentations button on the top-left corner. This will transfer the screen to the Presentations view.

Once done, as you can see from Fig 2, you will be presented with a host of themes to choose from (there may be more than the screen can hold, so scroll to see the full choice). Some themes will provide subjects based on neutral backgrounds in order to give your work prominent display, while others will give you a graphical helping hand. When you are happy with your choice, tap the theme that you want.

When selected, the presentation opens with a thumbnail slide being posted on the left in the slide navigator section. Tap in the bottom-left corner of the screen to add a new slide (Fig 1) and edit by tapping the screen and entering text.

Fig 1: Pinching and zooming takes you into the image, providing a close-up of your chosen area

# "Moving or navigating around your presentation is intuitive"

## Presentation navigation

Moving or navigating around your presentation is intuitive but does require an initial period of adjustment. There are a variety of finger movements and touch sequences that will speed up your creative process. For example, selecting items on the screen can be done via tapping. This involves quickly and firmly touching the screen. When you lift the finger the action is completed.

When one finger isn't enough, you can use two. This is an ideal way to, for example, select an entire paragraph of text. The 'pinch and zoom' action has been associated with Apple ever since the iPhone hit the streets. Place two fingers on the screen and spread them apart. This zooms into the area of your choice (Fig 1). You can even increase the image size up to Full Screen or Maximum (200 per cent).

Reverse the process in order to bring the image to the default size. This gesture is also used to stop the playback of a presentation. To see items that are currently beyond the edges of the screen, just slide a finger along the screen in the desired direction (Fig 2). When playing a presentation, simply swipe to the left in order to move forward to the next slide or right to return (Fig 3).

Fig 2: If you then slide your finger along the screen, it will move the screen in your chosen direction

Fig 3: Flick your fingers along a crowded slide bar to see what lies off the screen

## Use the slide navigator cameras
### Move your slides as a set

### 1: Touch and drag
Touch and hold a slide until it rises and then drag it to the right.

### 2: Select your slides
While still holding the first slide, tap the other slides you want to move.

### 3: Select location
Drag the set to the desired location within the slide navigator.

### 4: Secure position
When you've positioned the set of slides, lift your finger from the screen.

**Text and graphics**
You can add text and graphics to the slide to give your creation an individual look

**Image**
Tap on the icon to swap the current image with one in your archive

**Slideshow scroll**
Scroll through the small, thumbnail images, within the slide navigator, in order to select your screen of choice

**Text replace**
You will need to double-tap the text box in order to edit your text

## App compatibility

It is possible to save time, when adding text to your presentations by copying that text from other apps such as Pages, Safari, Numbers and Mail. Moving the text is very easy, taking just a few seconds to complete. Let's take Safari as a common example. Open the app and access the web page from which you would like to copy text. In this case, we have selected a page on sport in Wikipedia.

To begin the copy process, simply press your finger onto the area you would like to copy. A magnifying glass will then appear highlighting one or more words. Remove your finger from the screen and a blue, highlighted word(s) will remain along with two movable tags (Fig 1). Press, with the tip of your finger, on any of the tags in order to move and, making sure you keep your finger pressed, slide the tag and then extend it to

your required text selection. You will see that the newly selected text will be encompassed within the blue area. A Copy option will then appear (Fig 2). Press the Copy button. You then need to exit the Safari app and open the Keynote app. Select a screen to insert the text into. Press your finger on a piece of empty screen space and then a Paste button will appear. Press the Paste button to paste the selected text onto the screen (Fig 3).

*Fig 1: The first word selection can then be expanded by the judicious use of the tags, either side of the word*

*Fig 2: Everything within the blue box is copied to memory, ready to be pasted later*

*Fig 3: The pasted text can be edited and manipulated to better fit the slide of choice*

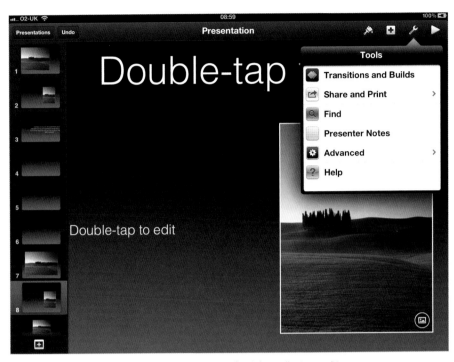

*Fig 1: When the Presenter Notes screen appears, the keyboard pops up from below to allow instant editing*

# "The slide that holds the Presenter Notes will be seen in the thumbnail area"

## Add Presenter Notes to a slide

When editing a slide, tap the spanner icon, situated on the top right-hand corner of the screen. A drop-down menu will appear. Tap the Presenter Notes button to open the utility. Once Keynote has switched to the Presenter Notes mode, you can then type your notes into the Presenter Notes area (Fig 1). As you type, the area scrolls down. If you type a web address, Keynote creates a hyperlink and treats it like any hyperlink on a slide.

To act as a reminder, the slide that holds the Presenter Notes will be seen, within the thumbnail area, with a yellow, turned-down corner (Figs 2 and 3). This is only visible while you're in Presenter Notes mode. Then, when you are ready, you can tap another slide in the slide navigator to type further presenter notes.

Meanwhile, it might be a good idea to keep an eye on the slide you are referring to within your notes. If you want to preview that slide, tap the right pointing arrow at the top of the screen to view the slide, and then double-tap anywhere on the screen to return to your Presenter Notes. If you want to add a new slide as a placeholder, and immediately begin typing notes for that slide, tap the plus icon at the bottom to add the slide, and then type.

*Fig 2: As soon as you start typing, the associated thumbnail icon features a turned down corner as a reminder reference*

*Fig 3: Ending the editing reveals that the thumbnail reminder can be plainly seen for future reference*

## Add animations
### Feature simple transitions in your slides

### 1: Transitions menu
Select a slide, tap Transitions and Builds from the Tools menu.

### 2: Access the effects
Tap the transition effect name. Scroll to see all the transition styles.

### 3: Select an option
Tap Options to customise the transition and choose when you want it to start.

### 4: Tap Done
When you've finished setting up transitions, tap Done in the top-right.

# GarageBand

GarageBand allows you to record, edit and share your musical creations without touching a Mac or PC. Whether you're an absolute beginner or professional musician, this app is for you

## Use it to:

- **Play virtually**
  Play a range of realistic touch-based instruments.

- **Play smartly**
  Let GarageBand do the hard work for you.

- **Multi-track record**
  Tie it all together for the perfect tune.

- **Have jam sessions**
  Connect with other iPads to play with friends.

- **Get iCloud integration**
  Start work on one device; finish off on another.

- **Export easily**
  Send your tracks to iTunes, Facebook and more.

- **Get mic support**
  Record real instruments.

*Fig 1 (top left): Every GarageBand tune starts by creating a song in the My Songs interface*

*Fig 2 (main image): Instrument settings are the key to finding an individual sound*

*Fig 3 (bottom left): There are plenty of instruments to choose from and to be customised*

# Music made easy

Turning your musical ideas into reality is easy with GarageBand

## Make a catchy song with no musical knowledge

Although GarageBand is used by professional musicians to demo their ideas while they're on the road or in the studio, it really comes into its own when it's used by the rest of us who don't know a great deal about recording music or playing instruments. To get started, just create a new song in the My Songs view (this loads by default when the app is started), select your instrument from the Instruments menu and get creative (see Figs 1 and 2).

The beauty of GarageBand comes from its flexibility; once you've found an instrument you want to use to start your song with, you can stick to the default settings, which sounds fairly true to life, or adjust every option until you've got the perfect sound you're after – it's really up to you (Fig 3). If you're fairly confident, every software instrument should provide you with enough creative freedom, but if you're feeling like you need a little help, it's best to select one of the smart instruments (they have a cog surrounding their icon) which can assist you by completing chords or even completely playing themselves based on the musical key and settings you choose.

Over the next few pages, we'll take you through what each of these instruments do and how they can add life to your sound.

Fig 1: Each live drum kit is set up exactly like its real counterpart, making it easy to play straight away

# "It's surprisingly intuitive and you'll soon be laying down the perfect beat"

## Drums

No matter what genre you work with, it's unlikely that any song you record on your iPad will be without a great drum track, and GarageBand offers a few amazing kits. Select drums from the Instruments menu and you'll be presented with the Classic Studio Kit by default. Getting some sounds out of it is as simple as tapping the drums you'd like to play. It's surprisingly intuitive and even if you've never touched a drum kit before, you'll soon be laying down the perfect beat (Fig 1).

It doesn't end with the Classic Studio Kit though; if your sound requires something

different, tap on its name above the toms and you'll be presented with six kit options to choose from: Classic Studio Kit, Vintage Kit, Live Rock Kit, Classic Drum Machine, House Drum Machine, and Hip Hop Drum Machine (Fig 2). Each kit has its own merits, but it's fair to say that if you're looking for a live sounding track then the first three should do the trick, whereas the drum machines work better on electronic-style songs. Each kit can be customised and configured in the settings menu which controls how sensitive they are to different velocity hits and whether the kick drum plays with the cymbal or not (Fig 3).

Fig 2: Choose from a total of six drum kits, each with a totally dynamic and different sound

Fig 3: Drum sounds can easily be controlled and customised from the settings menu to get things exactly how you like them

## Swipe and tap
For perfect recordings, know the basics of editing

### 1: Tap and select a track
Tap once on any track in arrangement view to select it for editing.

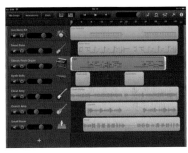

### 2: Drag and trim it
Drag the handles at either end of the track to trim the end or beginning.

### 3: Extra options
Double-tapping any track will bring extra options such as cut, split or delete.

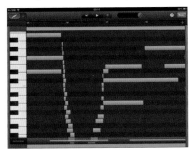

### 4: Open the piano roll editor
In the extra options menu, tap Edit to bring up the advanced piano roll editor.

## Change the scale

The controls on the far-left above the keys set the octave (the pitch) that's in use on the keyboard

## Swipe or play

The button in the centre above the keys sets whether swiping across them plays a glissando or changes the octaves

## Instrument controls

The main panel in the keyboard's interface controls the different settings for that specific instrument, more so for electronic sounds

## Too many keys?

The button on the far right sets the key size on screen and toggles velocity sensitivity to tweak the sound

## Keyboards

If you're looking to add layers to your track, look no further than keyboards. There are 48 different types to choose from in GarageBand, each with vastly different sounds to help you sculpt your song (Figs 1, 2 and 3).

On the far right, above the keys themselves, is the Keyboard button. Tap this to view a number of options to help you customise both the interface and the sounds that it produces. You can choose how many keys are visible on-screen and how wide they are. The single octave view doesn't give you such a high range but helps for a note-perfect performance by increasing individual key sizes. On the other hand, the two-octave layout allows you to easily play two-hand pieces.

Elsewhere in the Keyboard menu, you can toggle velocity sensitivity, so harder taps produce stronger sounds, and choose whether swiping your finger up and down the keyboard will produce a glissando or move the octave up or down. Above these options is the specific keyboard settings, and these can be tweaked to produce the perfect sound for your song, especially with the organs. Master the keyboards and you'll be well on your way to creating a great track.

## "There are 48 types of keyboards in GarageBand, each with vastly different sounds to sculpt your song"

Fig 1: GarageBand's keyboards are fairly true to life and easily manipulated for any song or genre

Fig 2: GarageBand's keyboard selection is the most expansive out of every instrument available within the app

Fig 3: The synth sounds in GarageBand are easily the most versatile and flexible in terms of replicating other instruments

*Fig 1: You can instantly manipulate any guitar sound with a selection of two different stompbox effects*

# "With each bass and guitar type, you can choose to play notes or chords"

## Guitars and bass

Guitars and bass in GarageBand are what adds that much-needed melody and final touch to your songs. Unlike the other instruments, these only come in Smart Instrument form – however, they're still more than capable of creating some amazing sounds (Fig 1).

There are four different guitar types to choose from: Acoustic, Classic Clean, Hard Rock and Roots Rock; and eight basses, the majority of which have a fairly similar interface. With each bass and guitar type you can choose whether you'd like to play notes or chords (with notes, you can also choose the scale you'd like to play in), the Autoplay level, and add effects (Fig 2).

Without Autoplay, playing chords is as simple as tapping on the different chord names or individual strings, but with Autoplay on, individual strings disappear and tapping on chord names instructs GarageBand to play riffs for you (Fig 3). There are four different Autoplay modes, all producing different results, so take your time to pick and choose the right one for your song. Try layering up different guitar and bass sounds for some truly amazing musical results reminiscent of rock legends Queen and Led Zeppelin.

*Fig 2: When playing individual notes, GarageBand lets you select different scales to help you nail that all-important solo*

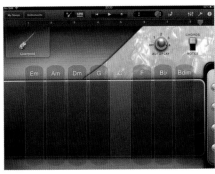

*Fig 3: Turning on Autoplay removes individual strings, making it easier to create basics riffs from chords*

# Export your song
## If you want to do some editing, export it to your Mac

### 1: Select the right song
Head into My Songs, hit the edit button then select the song to export.

### 2: Choose sharing setting
Tap the sharing settings icon and select 'iTunes' from the list.

### 3: Select a file type
To preserve editing capabilities, export the song as a GarageBand file.

### 4: Send it wirelessly
If you're not editing your track and want to send it as an audio file, select Mail.

## Add loops
Here's how to use loop files on your tracks

### 1: Tap the 'loops' icon
Tap the 'loops' icon in the top-right corner of the multitrack view interface.

### 2: Tap to preview any loop
Tap on a loop in the list to preview its sound. Tap again to pause it.

### 3: Search for your favourites
If you have a particular loop in mind, use the search bar to find it.

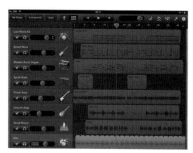

### 4: Drag it into multitrack
Once you've chosen a loop, drag it into a blank space in the multitrack view.

## Track controls
Across the top bar of the multitrack view is GarageBand's track controls – these play, pause, record or rewind the song and more

## Different tracks
Each instrument has its own track in the multi-track view. Waveforms show when music is being played by each one

## Sampler
If you're looking for a truly unique sound to add to your song, then look no further than GarageBand's sampler. It's more than just a simple way to replay recorded sounds. The sampler in this app actually allows you to completely manipulate recordings and play them back at different pitches using GarageBand's keyboard interface.

In order to get to work with the sampler, start off by recording your sound by hitting the big red Start button. Once you've done that it'll be added to a bank of recorded samples for you to edit and replay (Fig 1). In the sample editor, you can trim your recording to only use a certain part of it (great for longer field recordings), reverse it, detune it and change the shape of the sound altogether (Fig 2). It's easy to get carried away with this and ruin your recordings, so there's a revert button in the top-right. But sometimes this experimentation can lead to some truly unique sounds that can really raise the standard of your recording.

Once you've tweaked your recorded sample, all that remains is for you to play it out using the keyboard as you would on any other regular instrument. Notes won't always play out as expected, but that's the beauty of this wonderfully unique GarageBand for iPad tool.

Fig 1: The start of every great sampler sound involves recording a sample to be manipulated and played out

Fig 2: GarageBand offers some extensive editing options for recorded sounds to make for some truly unique sampler results

Fig 1: Smart String arrangements are easy to set up – just tap the instruments you'd like to use

# "For rhythm without effort, Smart Drums allows you to cook up a beat"

## Smart instruments

We've already touched on Smart Instruments with smart guitars and basses, but the latest addition to GarageBand for iPad is Smart Strings – and they're so versatile that they deserve a section for themselves.

Fire up Smart Strings and you're presented with a string quintet, based upon real orchestral recordings to work with (Fig 1). As you'd expect, the sounds you'll get out of Smart Strings are hugely realistic, so there's no reason why you shouldn't experiment and include them in your songs. Like smart guitars and basses, smart strings work in much the same way, allowing you to play

both individual notes or chords, or even have GarageBand play for you thanks to the Autoplay feature. All of this can be set up in seconds, giving more time to focus on your arrangements. Tapping on any of the stringed instruments will remove them from the arrangement, giving you the choice between a solo cello or the orchestra force of a full quintet – it's completely up to you (Fig 2).

For rhythm without effort, GarageBand includes Smart Drums, allowing to you cook up a beat without the need for sense of timing (Fig 3). Just drag the different drums onto the diagram and have GarageBand play them for you – setup takes just a few seconds.

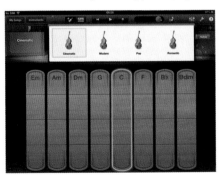

Fig 2: Choose from four different orchestra types in order to ensure the perfect sound for your song

Fig 3: GarageBand's Smart Drums are probably the easiest of all instruments to set up in the app

## Master controls
### Know exactly how to control each track in the mix

### 1: Drag from the left
Drag the handle next to the track icons to the right to reveal their controls.

### 2: Fix the volume mix
Each track has a volume slider, allowing you to mix your project to perfection.

### 3: Solo the important ones
Tap the headphones icon next to each track name to listen in solo mode.

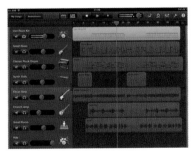

### 4: Mute the bad tracks
To mute a track, tap the speaker icon. It glows blue when active.

# iMovie

iMovie is one of the latest additions to the iLife catalogue of apps designed for iOS devices. It is a simple movie-editing suite that allows you to turn HD video into a trailer or masterpiece

## Use it to:

- **Create trailers**
  Edit your movies to look like movie trailers.

- **Add photos to video**
  Add photos from your iPad's camera roll to your movies.

- **Add music**
  Add music from your library to enhance your video.

- **Use different themes**
  Choose from eight themes to give your movies a different look.

- **Share online**
  Share your video clips through a number of social networks.

- **Link your Apple TV**
  Use Apple TV to stream your movies on your HDTV.

*Fig 1 (top left): Tap the music icon followed by the theme music to open up the song choices*

*Fig 2 (main image): Tapping on the gear icon opens the simple options window. Swipe to view the different icons*

*Fig 3 (bottom left): View the style used for banner text by navigating to that point*

# Create a film

Create a simple video project using the iMovie app

### Make a movie from eight themes

Making a video with iMovie can be as simple or in depth as you choose, by altering the finer settings to ensure the movie turns out just how you want it.

iMovie comes with eight built-in themes that give your movie a different look each time. The different themes can simply alter what the text banner looks like, change the background music of your movie, and give a different transition animation between clips (see Figs 1 and 3).

Switching between themes can be done at any point, even when you have finished putting together the footage – useful if you want to experiment with your movie theme after you have finished creating it.

To access the theme options, simply navigate to the options icon in the top right of the screen, as can be seen in the image above (Fig 2). Tapping on this will bring up a range of options, including the eight different themes and some simple options that will alter the theme you have selected. Swiping through the list allows you to browse the available themes and select the one you wish to use and that will fit to your movie. Tapping on a chosen theme will instantly apply it to your project, altering the settings to match the theme options you have chosen.

*Fig 1: By double clicking on a specific section of video, you are offered text options, allowing you to add text and adjust its positioning*

# "Adding a title to your movie will let viewers know what they're watching"

## Titles and transitions

Adding a title to your movie can be useful to label the clip, let viewers know what they are watching, and give the video an identity.

Adding a title is simple and is customisable in a number of ways. To add a title, simply double-tap on the section of the movie you'd like to add it to. This will bring up a small window where you can select a number of options for your text. Using the on-screen keyboard, you can then simply type your title into the box directly onto the video (Fig 1).

To help seamlessly merge different video clips, iMovie will automatically apply a transition animation between clips. By navigating to a break in your project and tapping on the black arrow symbol, it is possible to touch the yellow arrow symbol to break apart the movie. From here you can slide the individual movie clips left and right to adjust the transition point (Fig 2). For the transition animation, you can select the default dissolve option, or choose one bespoke to your particular theme. As well as this, it is possible to adjust the time of the transition between video clips, allowing you to fully customise it to suit your personal preferences (Fig 3).

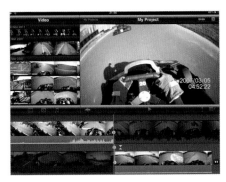

*Fig 2: With the movie clips separated, you can simply slide them to adjust their start and finish points*

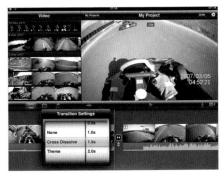

*Fig 3: Using the options window you can select the type of transition as well as the duration of the animation*

## Import footage
Import video clips from your camera roll to your project

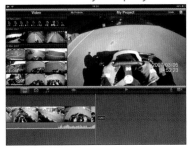

### 1: Select the video tab
Tap on the video icon. This will open up the available videos on your iPad.

### 2: Select a clip
Tapping on a video clip will highlight it to show you which you have chosen.

### 3: Trim it to size
Using the small yellow dots, drag in to trim the video down.

### 4: Import into project
When happy, tap the arrow or drag the video to import it into your project.

# iMovie

**Available files**
All of the available files, including pictures, music and videos found on your iPad can be found here ready to import

**Theme options**
The options icon allows you to browse the eight available themes as well as edit some of the basic options

**Project**
Your project timeline is displayed along the bottom of the interface where you can view and edit individual clips of video

**Preview panel**
The preview panel allows you to preview the movie so far, as well as act as a quick edit screen when trimming video clips

## Cut a trailer

One of the main features available with iMovie is the ability to create cinematic movie trailers. Upon opening the iMovie application, the '+' symbol allows you to start a new project or trailer. Selecting a new trailer takes you to the trailer development screen where you can preview pre-made trailers and select your theme (Fig 1). Once you've chosen a theme,

simply tap 'create' to launch the editor. From inside the editor you will be able to follow a simple step by step guide, filling in the necessary information about the trailer (Fig 2).

The next step of the process sees you selecting short clips of video to use within the trailer (Fig 3). Each different section of the trailer is demonstrated with a simple template, allowing you to select short clips of videos to

best suit the trailer. Tapping on the different videos available shows a small outline with the length of clip you're able to use. Tapping the arrow symbol will insert that clip into place. Within the same process are a number of text fields, each of which represent text displayed during the trailer. Simply tapping on these allows you to edit the text to best suit the needs of your video clips.

*Fig 1: The opening trailer screen allows you to preview the different themes and select the one suited to your movie clips*

*Fig 2: The first step takes you through the process of adding the necessary text, including the title and credits*

*Fig 3: The final stage takes you through adding small video clips to fill the necessary gaps of the trailer*

Fig 1: By tapping on the black arrow icon, the smaller yellow icons reveal that the precision editor can be opened for fine tuning

# "Edit different video clips together to allow for accurate, seamless transitions"

## Precision editor

The precision editor allows you to carefully edit the different video clips together to allow for an accurate, seamless transition.

With more than one clip imported into the project, the transition between the two is done via a small animation. Locate the timeline to the transition point. There is a small arrow icon that signifies where this is. When you tap on this, it will become highlighted, with another small arrow icon appearing below (Fig 1). From here it is possible to use a pinching motion with two fingers to open up the precision editing section, or alternatively,

by tapping on the new arrow icon (Fig 2). With the precision editor now open you can simply slide the two video clips from side to side to accurately place the start and finishing points, as well as the transition point between the two (Fig 3). This allows for pinpoint precision editing, ensuring every step of your movie is produced exactly how you want it.

Once you have completed the editing process and are happy with the results, simply pinch to close the precision editor, or touch the yellow arrow icons. This will return the timeline to its original state, having saved the changes you have made.

Fig 2: Using the pinching motion, the precision editor can be opened up below the original video clip

Fig 3: Double tap the separation block to open the transition settings and choose the animation and length of transition

## Use sound effects
Add simple sound effects to enhance your video

### 1: Tap on music icon
Tapping on the music icon brings up different sound options.

### 2: Navigate sound effects
Browse through the different sounds to find one that 'fits' your movie.

### 3: Tap to insert into timeline
From within the sound menu tap the 'Play' icon to preview the effect.

### 4: Adjust settings
Double tapping on a sound clip gives options to adjust volume and length.

# iMovie

## Add photos
### Add photos to make your movie more dynamic

### 1: Add photo to timeline
View images from your camera roll and tap on one to add it to your project.

### 2: Select image
Tapping on the image within the timeline will highlight it as a selection.

### 3: Select end position
With the image selected, pinch, zoom and drag the image to select the end.

### 4: Select start position
With the end position selected, repeat the steps to choose the start position.

### Timeline
With the precision editor open it's easy to ensure all of the items on the timeline are lined up precisely, including the transition period and sound clips

### Image palette
With the image palette open, you can simply scroll through your camera roll to see the photos available to add to your project

## Use AirPlay to stream to TV
Playing back your movie clips and trailers doesn't have to be restricted to simply viewing them on your iPad. Using AirPlay, it is possible to stream your movies through Apple TV to view it directly on your HDTV.

Once you have completed editing and formatting your movie and are ready to view the video, simply return to the main screen where all of your projects are displayed. From here you have a number of options, including exporting your video to your Camera Roll, sharing it online through a number of social networking sites or simply playing the movie in full screen on your iPad (Fig 1). When the video begins to play, the usual pause and skip controls will be displayed along the bottom, along with a symbol for AirPlay (Fig 2).

Tapping this icon will take you to the main screen where it will begin to prepare the movie for AirPlay. The video will then be mirrored on your HDTV and appear as it would do on the iPad, allowing you to experience the movie you've just created on a much larger and traditional format, while all the time being able to control it using the iPad interface.

Fig 1: The main project screen allows you to simply press the 'play' icon to launch a full screen preview of the movie

Fig 2: Once the video starts playing, the AirPlay icon will appear along with the other controls

Fig 1: Once in the correct position on the timeline, simply selecting the video recording icon will take you into the device's video camera

# "It is possible to film video clips from within the iMovie application and instantly insert them into your project timeline"

## Film from within the app

It is possible to film video clips from within the iMovie application and instantly insert them into your project timeline. This is helpful if there is extra footage that needs to be added to the project, or even a small space that needs to be filled, avoiding the need to use the camera application and insert the footage.

With the correct position selected in the project timeline, simply press the video recording button to jump straight into the video camera (Fig 1). This window acts in the same way as the device's camera application,

allowing you to select either the still camera or the HD video camera to record new media to insert into your movie (Fig 2).

From here you are able to record as normal, before being given the option to replay your footage and retake it if you aren't happy with it. However, if you choose to insert it into your movie, simply tap 'Use' and it will be placed in the position in the timeline that was last selected (Fig 3). From here it is then possible to carry out generic edits to the video footage, such as adjusting the transition details and adding some text.

Fig 2: The video camera works in the same way as the camera app, allowing you to use either camera and shoot video or stills

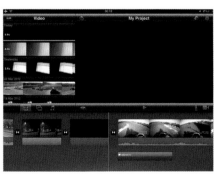

Fig 3: Once the video has finished recording, tapping 'Use' will simply insert it into your movie timeline

## Camera roll exports
Export movies and trailers to your iPad's camera roll

### 1: Project screen
Navigate to the main screen where you can view your finished movie projects.

### 2: Export movie
Tap the Export button at the base of the screen, for different exporting options.

### 3: Video quality
Selecting Camera Roll offers a choice of different formats for varied video quality.

### 4: Prepare video
Once selected the film will be processed and exported to your camera roll.

# iPhoto

Along with the announcement of the new iPads in 2012, Apple revealed its latest iOS app, iPhoto. Editing, organising and sharing your images is now a whole lot easier on your iPad

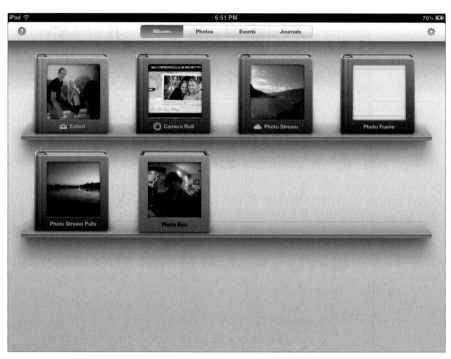

## Use it to:

- **Fix photos**
  Remove blemishes and red-eye with a tap.

- **Add filters and effects**
  Add various filters and effects using Swatch Book.

- **Use multi-touch**
  The app is designed to specifically take advantage of the iPad's multi-touch interface.

- **Beam photos**
  You can send photos quickly to other iOS devices using Beam.

- **Create Journals**
  Create and share photo collages called Journals.

- **Edit without fear**
  You can return your photos to their original state at any time.

*Fig 1 (top left): You can scroll through individual photos as well as Albums and Events*

*Fig 2 (main image): Individual Albums, Events and Journals are shown as books sitting on shelves on the screen*

*Fig 3 (bottom left): Tap and hold to compare images. Swipe to remove them*

# Edit and organise your photos
## Use multi-touch to improve your photos and share them with friends

### Smart browsing

One of the best things about the new iPhoto app is the way it helps with the organisation of your photos. The app sorts your photos into groups, with Camera Roll being placed in one 'book' and other sources of photos, such as Photo Stream, Albums, Events and Edited photos taking up different areas on the virtual shelves (see Fig 2). You can access your photos by simply tapping on the area you want, or by swiping between sections (Fig 1).

When you're browsing your photos in the single photo view, there are other great ways to view them. Hold your finger down on one photo and then another, for example, and you can compare them directly. You can continue to add photos to the comparison, and remove them by swiping them downwards and off the screen (Fig 3).

Touch and hold on two photos at once and you will select those two and every one in between, giving you a range to view. Finally, you can double-tap any image and iPhoto will scan through the album you're viewing and bring up any photos that are similar. This is fantastic if you're trying to find the best image to edit. All of these editing gestures make finding the right photo a lot simpler.

Fig 1: Tap and hold with two fingers and this lens will appear to view close detail on an image

# "Apple has worked hard to ensure iPhoto uses natural multi-touch gestures"

## Multi-touch editing

Because Apple developed the new iPhoto app alongside the new iPad, it worked hard to ensure that it used as many natural, multi-touch gestures as possible. The result is an app that utilises gestures in all the ways you would imagine, and several that you would never have thought of.

While some of the gestures, such as pinching to zoom or crop, and twisting two fingers to straighten the photo are fairly basic, others are truly inspired. Tapping and holding two fingers on the screen when viewing individual images will bring up a zoom ring

that allows you to focus on a specific area of the photo. You can drag this around with your finger to get a closer look at different areas of the photo and then twist the lens with two fingers to zoom in even further (Fig 1).

The whole app includes fantastic features like this, whether it's a simple case of touching on the area of the photo you want to edit and dragging a finger, or physically tipping your iPad left and right to straighten up the image (Figs 2 and 3). You might have used editing software on your iPad before, but this makes the most of the hardware to create something that is a genuine joy to use.

Fig 2: In the Crop section, place two fingers on the screen and you can rotate and straighten your photo

Fig 3: Tap and drag in the Colour mode and you can alter the colour of whatever is under your finger

## Adjust the brightness
Brighten up your darker images with a swipe

### 1: Exposure controls
Choose the Exposure control (aperture icon) from the icons in the bottom left.

### 2: Tap and hold
Place a finger on the screen. Arrows allow you to change exposure settings.

### 3: Drag
Drag your finger up from its starting point to increase brightness.

### 4: At the bar
Alter the colour settings using the bar along the bottom of the screen.

iPhoto

**Photo browser**
Your photos can be viewed on the left-hand side of the screen, but can be dragged off screen with your finger

**Edit button**
In the top-right of the screen is the Edit button. Tap this to start altering your photo

**Sharing**
The Sharing options sit at the top of the screen and include a range of choices for letting others see your photos

**Tools**
In the bottom-left are your tools. You can choose to apply as many as you like by tapping them

## The swatch book

One of the things that iPhoto does best is add special effects and filters to your photos (Fig 1). You can access a swatch book that fans up from the bottom of the screen and contains a selection of different filters that you can apply to your image (Fig 2).

This swatch book acts as more than a way to access the effects, however. Each swatch represents a category of filters and effects, such as Black & White. When you choose one of the swatches it stays at the bottom of the screen for you to choose the specific type of effect you want. You can tap between the different effects and see the changes appear instantly on the photo above (Fig 3).

Thanks to the way iPhoto deals with these edits, nothing is lost as you apply various effects and colour corrections. The Undo button sits at the top of the screen at all times to let you quickly remove something you don't like and return to the previous state.

If you want to go right back to the start you can easily do this as well. Simply, tap the cog that's located in the bottom right, and you can choose to remove all effects and return the image to its original state so you can start manipulating your image all over again.

*Fig 1: Tap the Effects button in the bottom left of the screen to bring up the choices for edits*

*Fig 2: The swatch book that fans open will show you small previews of the image with each effect*

*Fig 3: For effects such as vignette, you can pinch with two fingers to move and resize the effect*

Fig 1: Tap the Brushes icon in the bottom left of the screen to bring up this fan of different brushes

# "Apply effects to a small area of the photo by simply brushing with your finger"

## Brushes

Another fantastic way of editing your photos on your iPad is by using Brushes in iPhoto (Fig 1). The tools on offer enable you to alter everything from the saturation to the contrast. What's particularly brilliant about this part of the app, however, is that you can apply these effects to just a small area of the photo by brushing on it with your finger.

For example, if you want to repair a small area of the photo that is blemished, or fix red-eye caused by the flash of a camera, you can choose these brushes and just tap the areas

affected. The same goes for lightening an area of the photo; if you can't see a face because of a bright background, choose the brighten brush and you can paint over the darker area to pick out the details. The effect is obvious immediately (Fig 2), but you can increase the effect of the brush using the menu at the bottom (Fig 3). Zoom is handled with a pinch to get you more accuracy. You can also choose to see your strokes to pick up on any areas you've missed while applying the effect. It's a very powerful and extremely useful tool, more so once you're familiar with it.

Fig 2: You should see an immediate change as soon as you start painting your chosen effect onto a photo

Fig 3: Options are available in the bottom-right to show strokes and apply the effect to the whole image

## Social media sharing

Share your photo with friends using social media services

### 1: Sharing choices

Tap the Sharing button at the top of the screen for a list of options.

### 2: Flickr

Share your image to Flickr by logging into your account using this screen.

### 3: Twitter

Thanks to Twitter integration, you can tweet within iPhoto to your account.

### 4: Facebook

Facebook needs your permission before you can send any photos to it directly.

## Resize and crop
### Alter the size and shape of an image using your fingers

### 1: Horizontal
Tap Crop & Straighten and iPhoto will try to find the horizon to level your photo.

### 2: Cropping
You can use a finger to chop down your image, or pinch with two fingers.

### 3: Presets
Tap the cog for a range of preset sizes to choose from for fast resizing.

### 4: Accelerometer
To straighten the image, drag the wheel or tap it and tip your iPad.

### Album shelves
You can see your albums here with a cover photo for each. Grey albums are those you've created, while brown are the ones iPhoto creates

### Switching
You can switch between the different areas using the buttons at the top of the screen, or by swiping left and right

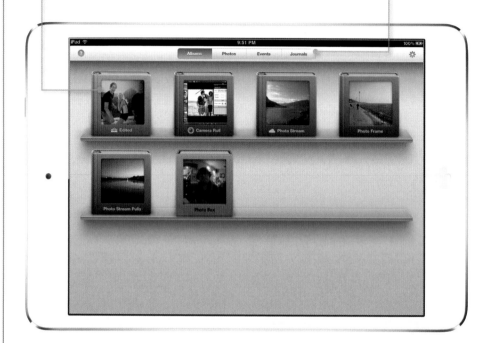

## Slideshows
While editing your shots is a huge part of using iPhoto, Sharing is also a massive part of what the app is about. You can share individual images with your friends online using a range of services that are built into the app, but it is also possible to share your images locally with a fantastic selection of slideshows.

They are incredibly easy to set up thanks to the Sharing button that stays constantly at the top of the screen. Tap it to see the slideshow option at the bottom, and you can then select the images you want to use, as well as the type of transitions you need (Fig 1).

There are plenty to choose from, and also handy options that include the ability to play music in the background (Fig 2).

These are a great way to share your photos if you're just passing your iPad around friends and family, but if you have an Apple TV you can also put the slideshow on the big screen and let people view it on there. Controls appear during the slideshow if you tap the screen, allowing you to pause on a photo you love or skip through the less interesting shots if you prefer. This is a fantastic way to share your snaps, and there are enough themes to match whatever photos you're displaying.

*Fig 1: Tap the Sharing button in the top corner and you'll see the slideshow button at the bottom of the menu*

*Fig 2: There is a range of slideshow types to choose from, so there's bound to be one that matches the theme*

Fig 1: Edit individual photos by dragging to resize, tapping to add a caption, or double-tapping to move it around in the frame

# "Journals allows you to add your photos into a collage-style grid"

## Photo Journals

One of the new features that Apple introduced with the iPhoto app for iPad was Journals, accessed via the Share button in the top right, which allows you to add your photos into a collage-style grid. This grid is customisable, with options to resize each photo so you can pick out your favourite and make it larger. Just tap the edit button to access these options (Fig 1).

You also have the ability to add other features into the Journals, and this is where the app really comes into its own. Information is pulled from your photos, such as the date they were taken and any location data that

exists. If you took your photos on your iPad or on an iPhone, location data will probably be included automatically.

The app will also look up the weather for the location, and you can add notes, quotes and even restaurant information to give a full summary of your trip. To add these features (and more), tap the plus sign at the top-right of the screen (Fig 2). When you're finished, you can share it with anyone you want. Just hit the Share button and then iCloud, and you'll get a web address where the journal is on display, and the whole thing - including all the extra maps and weather info - can be browsed by anyone you choose (Fig 3).

Fig 2: In Edit mode you can quickly drag in items such as maps, calendar information, or weather

Fig 3: Sharing your Journal is simple. Tap iCloud and you will be given a URL to share with friends and family

## Share your Journals
Share your journals with friends and family

### 1: Sharing options
Share your Journal in several ways, but the best - by far - is the iCloud option.

### 2: Publish
The Journal will be made, and a URL for the Journal's location will appear.

### 3: View in Safari
Tap View in Safari to preview the Journal. Tap images to view them larger.

### 4: Share link
In iPhoto, choose 'Tell a Friend' to share the link to your Journal via email.

# Essential accessories

iPad accessories can enhance the device in so many ways and build upon its core strengths to create flexible solutions

An iPad on its own is a very powerful device, but the addition of some accessories can turn it into a chameleon capable of providing entertainment for groups of people, replacing a laptop, and letting you achieve more than you ever dreamed of. All of the technology built into the iPad lets it work wirelessly with some accessories and fixed to others, so there are plenty of choices open to you. Consider carefully which accessories will work best for you, and try to avoid the temptation of buying too many. It's true to say that with the addition of a few carefully selected add-ons, your iPad could become the hub for most of your needs at home and when travelling.

We will answer some frequently asked questions in this guide, as well as highlight the benefits of each of the main accessory types and, hopefully in the process, give you the inspiration you need in order to enhance and expand your iPad experience. You do not need to spend a lot to get the most out of your iPad through accessories, and you could potentially get all of your money back by offloading inferior solutions that you have used in the past. As we said, the iPad is very powerful on its own, but add some clever accessories, and it becomes a productive monster with the ability to help you do everything you need to and more.

Safari    Mail    Settings    Photos    Music

# Apple TV

Apple TV is capable of bringing high-definition movies to your TV without any wires – and lots more options besides this

### What does it offer, and how does it work with my iPad?

Apple TV enables you to play HD films and ad-free TV programmes on your HDTV at home. You can just purchase them from the device and then play them. You can also stream movies in full HD, courtesy of Netflix. You'll need a Netflix account, but you can subscribe from the TV app itself. In terms of iPad connectivity, you can mirror and stream content from your iPad 2 or new iPad to your TV. You can show off your iPad photos on a big screen, play your iPad's music on your home speakers and even take advantage of dual-screen gaming on selected apps.

### Can I connect an Apple TV to a standard definition TV?

Although possible, Apple TV is only officially compatible with high-definition TVs and requires an HDMI cable to pass the signal through. There are many good reasons for this: the user experience would not be the same through standard definition, the rented movies are presented in 1080p HD, and it is difficult to ensure that all older standard definition TVs would be compatible with this. HDTVs subscribe to set standards to ensure that the experience is the same for everyone, and the Apple TV interface would not look half as good in lower resolution.

### The included remote control is very basic. Are there any alternatives available?

Your iPad can be used as a more advanced remote control if you choose to download the free Apple Remote app from the App Store. It is a visually pleasing tool, and will almost certainly fit the way you are using Apple TV in some circumstances. You can control AirPlay in many rooms, view album and movie artwork, as well as do so much more besides all of this.

The fact that the iPad keyboard can be used to find a title is much more convenient than trying to tap out the letters on the Apple TV interface – this facet alone makes it worth trying out. When you consider that there is also iCloud compatibility and simple gesture control included, your iPad will soon feel like a natural part of your Apple TV setup. There have been some reported quirks regarding how the app works, but it is almost always an excellent solution have.

> "With its simple gesture control, your iPad will soon feel like a natural part of your Apple TV setup"

## How to: Mirror your iPad video on Apple TV

**1: Get connected**
Ensure your iPad and Apple TV are connected to the same Wi-Fi network.

**2: Activate your iPad**
Double tap the home button and slide the recently used apps strip right.

**3: Enable mirroring**
Tap the TV icon, then select Apple TV and ensure that 'Mirroring' is on.

# Wireless keyboard

A wireless keyboard can turn an iPad into an efficient laptop replacement

### What is the best type of keyboard to use for my iPad?

This is very much dependent upon taste and an individual's particular needs, but try to go for one with the best keys possible. There are various types of iPad keyboards available which can either be completely separate from the iPad in use – housed in a case that also encloses the keyboard – and others that offer the kind of stability you would expect from a netbook when used on your lap. If possible, avoid keyboards with rubber keys, because these are only as effective as typing on a screen, and think carefully about how you would use your iPad with a keyboard attached. You will want a practical solution that works best for you and your needs.

### Will a wireless keyboard drain the battery on my iPad?

The drain from a keyboard attached via Bluetooth is very low in comparison to the amount of power the screen, Wi-Fi and processor need. In normal, everyday use, you will barely notice any extra battery drain from using a Bluetooth keyboard. Your main concern should be ensuring that the keyboard has enough power to keep working. They are usually charged by USB, and will almost certainly have less battery runtime than the iPad itself. When you choose a keyboard, try to get one with the longest battery life per charge, because this will make a big difference to how practical a solution it is for you, more so if you use it often.

### Is a completely separate wireless keyboard a more flexible solution for the iPad?

Not really. You can buy wireless keyboards that will work with the iPad and other devices, but you need to also consider exactly 'how' you would go about using it. Often it will make more sense to simply purchase a keyboard that allows the iPad to attach to it and to create a form that is comfortable to be used anywhere. You don't want to negate one of the iPad's greatest strengths by carrying a massive keyboard with it. As you will no doubt discover, keyboards that can attach to the iPad will almost certainly prove to be more flexible in the long run than those that remain completely separate.

> "In normal, everyday use, you will barely notice any extra battery drain from using a Bluetooth keyboard"

## How to: Install a keyboard on the iPad

### 1: Use the Bluetooth
Go to Settings and choose General> Bluetooth. Turn Bluetooth on.

### 2: Follow the instructions
Follow the instructions with the keyboard to activate the Discovery feature.

### 3: Recognition is complete
Both devices should now recognise each other.

# Headphones

The best way to enhance your iPad audio experience

### Will all makes of headphones work with the iPad?

In theory, almost every set of headphones should work with the iPad, but you should always check just in case you purchase a set that are specifically designed for another product. There are some non-Apple headphones on the market that have full compatibility with iOS devices. They enable you to skip tracks, fast forward and play/pause without having to touch the iPad. Be sure to check the packaging to see if these features are available in your chosen set.

### How much better are alternative headphones compared to the standard Apple set?

This answer to this is subjective, because the new Apple EarPods are actually very good, producing a vibrant and deep sound that most people will perceive to be excellent. However, if you are willing to spend more money, the difference in quality can be stark, thanks to the audio components used by the iPad, which are capable of delivering stunning sound through a good quality pair of headphones.

# Smart Cover

## A practical, good-looking and innovative accessory

### What's so special about the iPad Smart Cover?

Apart from its exceptionally good looks, it has some tricks up its sleeve which will become progressively more useful the more you use it. The clever magnet positioning means that you can simply attach it to the iPad by laying it on the front. You don't need to spend time positioning it because it will find the right place immediately. For those times when you are reading or watching a movie in bed, you can fold the back around to make a stand, which is a really convenient hands-free option. It will even automatically turn the iPad on and off. It is an ingenious solution, and a definite must-have accessory for any iPad user.

### Will a Smart Cover protect my iPad as well as a normal iPad case will?

The short answer is no, because it only protects the screen, and even then, only to a certain point. The cover is quite thin, and even though it attaches to the screen via magnets, it will not protect the screen if it is hit forcefully. The fact that the back is left exposed is the biggest cause for concern, however, and so you may want to either purchase a back cover that is compatible with the Smart Cover or a completely separate case for when you are travelling. The Smart Cover is fantastic in many ways, but is not a complete solution for every occasion.

### How can I properly clean the Smart Cover? Each side is made from different materials…

The front can be cleaned with anti-bacterial wipes or any wipes that do not contain excessive moisture. Always clean the cover away from the iPad in order to reduce the chances of dropping it or getting moisture onto the iPad itself. The inside coating is very different, and designed to protect the screen from scratches when closed, so try to avoid moist materials to clean it as far as you can. A light brushing with your hand or a thinly wired brush will usually be enough to clean off any marks or dust particles that have settled on it.

"You can fold the back around to make a stand, and it will even automatically turn the iPad on and off"

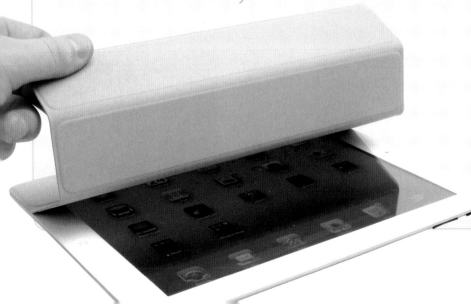

"Choose the best sounding speakers in the size range that fits you"

# Speakers

You can use wireless or docked speakers with an iPad to share the audio experience. There are almost too many choices out there!

### Does the size of the speakers I use matter when purchasing new ones?

Historically, the size of speakers has been directly proportional to the sound quality, but advances have meant that this is no longer completely true. There are speakers available now that are much smaller than the iPad, which can produce a loud and vibrant sound, but a set of high-end speakers that are larger will still likely offer the best sound of all. Think about your needs, and then choose the best sounding speakers in the size range that fits you. In most cases, this is an area where paying a little more will mean you reap a lot of audible benefits.

### Can I use my wireless speakers with other devices besides the iPad?

It completely depends on the kit, and it's worth considering before you purchase wireless speakers. It is worth thinking about how you may want to use a pair of wireless speakers, because some can also be used with TVs, games consoles and other products to increase the sound quality. When the iPad is connected they will still offer the same benefits, but some careful consideration could make them a multi-purpose solution for a variety of devices. Make sure you check out the range of speakers so you can get maximum flexibility out of them.

### Some speakers for the iPad are very expensive. Are they really worth the money?

If you play music a lot and store your entire collection on your iPad, then the answer is most likely a yes, but they don't just have to be a pair of speakers. There are plenty of models available that also act as bedside alarm clocks, and many come with remote controls to let you skip tracks from far away. Also, consider that a decent set of speakers could replace an entire stereo system and leave you with a solution that is used by the entire family. From this perspective, you start to see that the cost is not as prohibitive as it may have seemed at first.

## How to: Set the audio equalizer on an iPad

### 1: Find the settings
Go to Settings and tap the Music section. Upon doing this, you will see a selection of settings options pop up on the right-hand side.

### 2: Choose your mood
Tap 'EQ' and then choose an audio style from the list that comes up. You will need to experiment in order to find your preferred mood.

### 3: Set the volume
In this section you can also choose a volume limit, which is handy if your external speakers distort at a certain level.

# Printer

The days of fiddling around with printer drives and miles of cables are over. You now tap 'Print' and the magic happens automatically

## How do I know if a wireless printer will support my iPad for wireless printing?

Most printers that are compatible with an iPad for wireless printing will display AirPrint as a feature. However, not all that can support the iPad show this feature, so you may need to do some research to ensure that you buy one that works properly. Most AirPrint-compatible printers will also include wireless functionality that lets them work with other devices such as Windows and Mac desktops, so choose carefully and you will receive a one-for-all solution for all your printing requirements. Do this, and you may never need to go near a printer cable again.

## Are wireless printers easy to set up and configure on an iPad?

Check out our simple step-by-step guide below, but it's safe to say that in comparison to wired printers on desktops, which have long been a source of frustration for millions of people, it's child's play. There is no need to install extra software, provided you get a printer that is compatible. In most cases you will only need to tap the Print button on the iPad, and away you go. There will still be some configuration to do on the printer, such as connecting it to the right network, but besides that you can be assured that you will be up and running in minutes.

## How close do I need to be to the printer to make it work?

You can – believe it or not – be thousands of miles away, and still be able to print on some models. There are AirPrint-enabled printers that will let you email a document to them, and it will automatically print it for the people near the printer. But when in the same location, it will still accept prints from an iPad provided that both devices are within Wi-Fi range, which should still be a comfortable enough distance (depending on your router). The more you spend on a printer, the more flexibility you will have, but you'll be pleased to discover that there will rarely be a time when you cannot print wirelessly.

> "You'll be pleased to discover that there will rarely be a time when you cannot print wirelessly"

## How to: Set up printing on an iPad

### 1: Where are the settings?
Go to Settings and look for the printer options. As you will discover, there are none, simplifying things already.

### 2: Use an app
Open up an AirPrint-friendly app such as Pages, and select the print option from the menu that appears before you.

### 3: Print something
You can now select your printer, provided it's connected to the same Wi-Fi network. It's as simple as that.

> "Setting up printers on an iPad is child's play"

# Camera Connection Kit

The Camera Connection Kit is an ideal accessory for those who take pictures with a high-end digital camera. It's simple to use and works flawlessly

### Why would I need a Camera Connection Kit when I already have Photo Stream?

Simply due to the fact that only iOS devices are compatible with Photo Stream. This means that if you try to take pictures on a dedicated camera then you will find that there is no automatic method of moving photos to an iPad. This kit lets you insert an SD card into it, and when attached to the iPad the photos on the card will be viewable on the iPad. There is little delay when rendering the photos, and you can even adjust the photos and add effects straight away, and then share the results directly from the iPad.

### Will a Camera Connection Kit really save me time?

If you are a professional photographer - yes indeed! Imagine the scenario – you take some pictures with your DSLR camera, which are then stored on your camera's SD card. You will have to take that card and insert it into a card reader to copy or move the photos to a desktop or laptop computer. You then need to add them to your iPhoto library and sync the iPad to get the photos over to it. Now, the above method, and you can see that for

people who take lots of high-quality photos, this solution will save a lot of valuable time.

### What different image/video formats does the Camera Connection Kit support?

The kit supports a variety of popular formats, and, for most people, it will cover all of their needs. HD videos can be transferred using the kit, and even RAW photos are supported, which is ideal for professional photographers who need to show off or edit their work quickly. There will be some large photo types not supported, but these are usually required to be edited on a desktop anyway. For most people, however, the only concern will be the amount of available space on the iPad, as you may not want to keep all your photos on the iPad for an extended period of time.

## How to: Set up the Camera Connection Kit

**1: Two simple accessories**
Make sure you have both; the kit won't work without one.

**2: Connect one end**
Connect one end to the iPad and insert your SD card into the other.

**3: Direct to camera**
Use the second accessory to directly connect your camera to the iPad.

"The iPad Camera Connection Kit supports a wide variety of popular formats, and - for most people - it will cover all of their needs"

# Dock

### There are so many docks with numerous varied uses

**What's the most practical dock to use if I have some room to spare?**

The iPad Keyboard Dock enables you to charge and sync the iPad, while simultaneously acting as a desktop-capable keyboard for those times when you need to create longer documents. It looks stunning, fits the design of the iPad perfectly, and is incredibly useful for those who sometimes need to work from a static location.

### Can I dock and charge more than one device at a time?

There are docks available that will let you charge an iPad and an iPhone at the same time. This makes a lot of sense, because many iPad owners also own an iPhone, and doing this can also save space. Often, however, a dedicated dock just for the iPad will make for

## "A dedicated dock just for the iPad will make for an elegant solution"

a more elegant solution that lets you continue to work with it even when it is charging.

### Can a dock help me to undertake specific tasks or are they just for charging?

There are hundreds of docks available, many of which offer specific solutions for

entertainment and serious tasks. Some will turn the iPad into a retro gaming device, and there is even a dock that can take your blood pressure, as well as ones that can hang on the wall in order to turn your iPad into a live digital picture frame. You name the use, and the chances are there will be a dock that's available for it.

# Digital AV Adapter

### The Digital AV Adaptor is a simple accessory with so many uses

### Can I use the Digital AV Adapter with my television as well as a monitor?

As most televisions, monitors and projectors tend to have an HDMI input these days, the answer is most likely 'yes'. That said, it's always worth taking a look at the connections available to you before you go splashing out on this connection. Another caveat comes into play when it comes to mirroring content from different apps, although Apple's Digital AV Adapter does allow for full mirroring, some apps have disabled this, so check carefully.

### Why would I use this in place of the Apple VGA Adapter?

While the Digital AV Adapter may be an incredibly useful piece of kit, it comes undone when you're faced with older hardware that your iPad needs to interface with, such as older projectors or monitors. In this case, there's a very high chance that their main input connection will be VGA. That's where Apple's VGA adapter comes in. Our advice is

to always check the hardware you're planning on hooking up before you choose your AV accessories - long before the big presentation!

## "A flexible solution that will work with myriad display devices"

### What else can I use the Digital AV Adapter for?

Far from being a piece of kit reserved for stuffy business presentations, the Digital AV Adapter actually works best in the home, where showing off your favourite photos to a crowd of family and friends may not always be an option on the iPad's relatively small display. Hooking your iPad up to your TV is a great way to get those holiday snaps onto the big screen an ensuring no-one misses out on your the memories from your last trip.

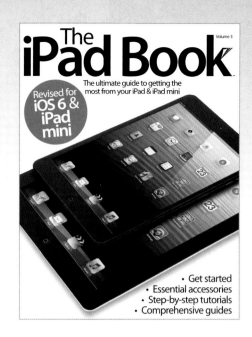